Shaykh Tusi

An Annotated Bibliography

The Mufid Academic Seminary is to be very greatly thanked for this annotated bibliography for Shaykh Ṭūsī. It is a superb contribution to the field of Islamic studies generally and Shī`ī studies in particular. The inclusion of references to Arabic and Persian-language secondary sources is especially welcome. This is an excellent follow-up to *Shaykh Mufīd, An Annotated Bibliography*. Both belong on any list of essential reference works! More please!

Professor Andrew J Newman
Personal Chair of Islamic Studies and Persian
Department of Islamic and Middle Eastern Studies
The University of Edinburgh

This is a very well extremely useful resource for all of us who study the history of Shiite Islam in general and Shaykh Tusi in particular. Careful, detailed and well-referenced, this will be an important resource for many years.

Professor Robert Gleave
Institute of Arab and Islamic Studies
University of Exeter

This is a much welcomed contribution to the studies of al-Shaykh al-Tusi, arguably the most innovative and towering Shiʿi thinker in the medieval period. The author does well to survey and annotate recent and not so recent works on al-Tusi's life, thought, and ideas in context. This work is a major development in the burgeoning sub-field of Shiʿi studies in Europe and will undoubtedly be of immense benefit to researchers and scholars in the field.

Dr. Ahab Bdaiwi
University Lecturer
Arabic and Medieval Philosophy
and Late Antique Intellectual History
School of Humanities
Leiden University

Shaykh Tusi

An Annotated Bibliography

Saleh A. Taleqani
Ali Deilamy Moezzi
Rasoul Naghavi

MUFID PRESS
2023

Mufid Academic Press
4000 Legato Road, Suite 1100, Fairfax, VA 22033
https://www.mufidseminary.org/

Published 2023.
Printed in the United States of America

ISBN: 9798850879754

Acknowledgments

This research was made possible with the supports of Mufid Academic Seminary. We thank Mohammad Baqir Kashmiri and Rasoul Naghavi for their support of the project. We also extend thanks to Yasser Pouresmaeil, Cyrus Zargar, and Mohammed Soori for their suggestions during the project. We appreciate Yasser Pouresmaeil and Mohammad Baqir Haghghani Fazl for their contribution in parts of the project. We also thank Mohammed Soori, Seyed Masoud Noori, Jerrmein Abu Shahba, Medina Talebi, and Kusmin al-Bekasi for contributing to the project. Finally, we thank a number of libraries (mentioned in the section of Methodology) which provided us with the main sources of the research.

Editors, Authors, and Contributors

Saleh A. Taleqani: Editor
Ali Deilamy Moezzi: Editor
Rasoul Naghavi: Editor-in-Chief
Sayyid Mohammad Baqir al-Kashmiri: Contributor
Cyrus Zargar: Contributor
Melanie G. Raza: Contributor in Part I
Yasser Pouresmaeil: Contributor in all Parts
Mohammad Baqir Haghghani Fazl: Contributor in Part 4

Table of Contents

Abbreviation and Key Words

Ṭūsī's works in this book are divided into five groups (with respect to the attribution of titles to Ṭūsī and the attribution of particular manuscripts to those titles). We have used the following attributions. The process through which these five groups are obtained is elaborated in the section on the Methodology.

A: Works with an available manuscript, where the attribution of the title to Ṭūsī and the attribution of the manuscript to the title are both accurate.

B: Works with an available manuscript, where the attribution of the title to Ṭūsī is accurate, but the attribution of the manuscript to the title is uncertain.

C: Works without an available manuscript, where the attribution of the title to Ṭūsī is accurate.

D: Works with an available manuscript, where the attribution of the title to Ṭūsī is uncertain, but the attribution of the manuscript to the title is accurate.

Note on Transliteration

As for transliterations, all names and terms are transliterated following the Arabic chart of IJMES (Cambridge University affiliated International Journal of Middle Eastern Studies). Here is the guideline:

https://www.cambridge.org/core/journals/international-journal-of-middle-east-studies/information/author-resources/ijmes-translation-and-transliteration-guide

As for bibliographies, we have followed the Chicago Manual of Style (here: https://www.chicagomanualofstyle.org/tools_citationguide/citation-guide-2.html, and for more details, see the links here: https://www.chicagomanualofstyle.org/home.html). Names and titles are transliterated as per the IJMES guideline but without diacritic marks, as it is permitted by the Chicago Manual of Style.

Preface

Ṭūsī (336-413 AH/948-1022) was a prominent Muslim theologian and jurist in the fifth century AH (eleventh century). Fifty-four works are attributed to him (see the section on Methodology, and Table II, for the accuracy or inaccuracy of such attributions), of which only 30 works are available, and 24 works are missing. His works are mainly about the following seven topics: theology, jurisprudence, hadiths, *rijāl* (evaluation of hadith transmitters), Quranic studies, principles of jurisprudence, and supplications.

Regarding the dominant themes of Ṭūsī's works, eighteen works are concerned with theology, fourteen works are concerned with jurisprudence, three works are concerned with *rijāl*, three works are concerned with hadiths, and the remaining sixteen are concerned either with other topics or a mixture of the aforementioned ones, as in the table below.

The present research pursues two goals: first, a descriptive bibliography of primary works by Ṭūsī, which are written by Ṭūsī himself, dictated by him, or selected from his works; second, a bibliography of recent (1970-2020) secondary sources about Ṭūsī and his works.

The book begins with a Methodology of this research, followed by four parts. The Methodology elaborates how the research into primary and secondary sources was carried out and how the references of the research are cited. Moreover, earlier bibliographies of Ṭūsī's works by other researchers are introduced.

Part I includes an introduction in which Ṭūsī's life is recounted—his life, education, migration to Baghdad, teachers, political circumstances of Baghdad since his migration until his religious leadership, his migration to Najaf, students, and writings.

Moreover, a chronology of crucial events in Ṭūsī's life and a chronology of his major works are presented in this part. Finally, we have provided a list of classical bibliographies of Ṭūsī.

Part II provides three lists: Ṭūsī in classical generations (*ṭabaqāt*), Ṭūsī in modern studies (1970-2020), and Ṭūsī in encyclopedia and dictionary entries.

Part III is an annotated bibliography of Ṭūsī's works, which is the main part of the book. There are eight general sections to this part, dealing respectively with: Ṭūsī's works in theology, jurisprudence, hadiths, *rijāl*, Quranic studies, principles of jurisprudence, supplications, and other works. Each of these sections ends with a list of Ṭūsī's missing works.

Part IV is a bibliography of secondary sources concerning Ṭūsī and his works. We have focused on sources written from 1970 to 2020. This part includes three general sections:

- A list of works in European languages (English, German, and French), where articles and dissertations about Ṭūsī are cited.
- Secondary sources in Arabic.
- And secondary sources in Persian, which are richer than the former two. In this last part, we have listed 181 books and articles about Ṭūsī.

For more about the primary and secondary works, see the section on Methodology.

Methodology

The Methodology for primary works (Authored by Ṭūsī)

This bibliography of Ṭūsī's work aims to provide a comprehensive list of all the works attributed to Ṭūsī in the following five sources to provide a self-sufficient bibliography of Ṭūsī's works. In cases where the attribution of a work to Ṭūsī is rejected or deemed questionable by certain scholars or the work in question is considered the same as another separately listed work by certain scholars and not by others, we do not make changes or eliminate the work from the list; instead, we keep the work on the list and point to the disagreements among the scholars. Thanks to a list provided by Ṭūsī of his own work, there is much less disagreement over the attribution of works to him than to his contemporaries such as Mufīd. For this reason, the list provided here is very close to previous bibliographies of Ṭūsī's work as far as the number and titles of his works are concerned. Still, our list has advantages over earlier bibliographies in its comprehensiveness by taking account of the most recent lists of manuscripts, including references to precise or approximate dates of some works, and reviewing accounts by different scholars.

To provide our list of Ṭūsī's work, we begin with a comprehensive list of his entire works as listed in the following five groups of sources:

1. *Al-Fihrist (The list)* by al-Shaykh al-Ṭūsī himself and *Rijāl* by al-Najāshī are the most reliable and earliest lists of Ṭūsī's works. Next is Ibn Shahrāshūb's *Ma'ālim al-'ulamā'*.

2. References to a work by Ṭūsī in another book. Sometimes Ṭūsī himself makes a reference to another work of his (e.g., a reference to his *al-Nihāya* in his *al-Ījāz fī l-farā'iḍ*), and sometimes another scholar attributes a book to Ṭūsī in his work or even cites materials from it (e.g., Sayyid Ibn Ṭāwūs cites *Hidāyat al-mustarshid* and *Baṣīrat al-muta'abbid* in his *Fatḥ al-abwāb*).

3. Recent biographies and bibliographies, such as *al-Dharī'a* by Āqā Buzurg Ṭihrānī and 'Āmilī's *A'yān al-Shī'a*.

4. Lists of manuscripts held by libraries. In this class, we have used lists of manuscripts in Iranian libraries and lists of online manuscripts at https://scripts.nlai.ir.

5. Recent research and papers dealing with Ṭūsī's work, including Āqā Buzurg Ṭihrānī's list in his biography and bibliography of Ṭūsī's work, and Adībīmihr's list and research concerning Ṭūsī's work.

In the next stage, we carried out a primary refinement of the list to remove repetitive works. We did not merge the works that appear with different titles on different lists, leaving their final judgement to the fifth stage when the research is completed. We merged the works with slight differences in their titles (such as *al-Junbalāniyya* and *al-Junbalā'iyya*), which were obviously identical.

In the third stage, we reviewed Ṭūsī's works as to availability or non-availability of their manuscripts, or as to the attribution of the manuscript in question to the title in question, or as to the attribution of the title in question to Ṭūsī, the upshot of which is as follows:

1. Availability of an alleged manuscript of the work

By an "alleged manuscript" we mean a manuscript claimed by Āqā Buzurg Ṭihrānī or other researchers after him to exist or appearing on lists of manuscripts, such as those of the Library of Ayatollah Mar'ashī

Najafī (in Qom, Iran) or *Fankha* (list of manuscripts in Iran). Here we face two questions:

(i) Is the attribution of the title in question to Ṭūsī accurate or inaccurate? There are three possibilities here: accurate, uncertain, and inaccurate.

(ii) Is the attribution of the alleged manuscript to the title in question accurate or inaccurate? Again, there are three possibilities here: accurate, uncertain, and inaccurate.

Thus, there will be nine possible states, as illustrated below. Some of these do not occur in our list, which will be italicized. (See also, Table I)

(1) The attribution of the title to Ṭūsī is accurate | the attribution of the manuscript to the title is accurate (**A**: accurate attribution/accurate attribution)

(2) The attribution of the title to Ṭūsī is accurate | the attribution of the manuscript to the title is uncertain (**B**: accurate attribution/uncertain attribution)

(3) The attribution of the title to Ṭūsī is accurate | the attribution of the manuscript to the title is inaccurate (*accurate attribution/inaccurate attribution*)

(4) The attribution of the title to Ṭūsī is uncertain | the attribution of the manuscript to the title is accurate (**D**: uncertain attribution/accurate attribution)

(5) The attribution of the title to Ṭūsī is uncertain | the attribution of the manuscript to the title is uncertain (*uncertain attribution/uncertain attribution*)

(6) The attribution of the title to Ṭūsī is uncertain | the attribution of the manuscript to the title is inaccurate (*uncertain attribution/inaccurate attribution*)

(7) The attribution of the title to Ṭūsī is inaccurate | the attribution of the manuscript to the title is accurate (*inaccurate attribution/accurate attribution*)

(8) The attribution of the title to Ṭūsī is inaccurate | the attribution of the manuscript to the title is uncertain (*inaccurate attribution/uncertain attribution*)

(9) The attribution of the title to Ṭūsī is inaccurate | the attribution of the manuscript to the title is uncertain (*inaccurate attribution/inaccurate attribution*)

2. An alleged manuscript of the title not available

(iii) Here again, the question arises: is the attribution of the title in question to Ṭūsī accurate or inaccurate? Again, there are three possible states here: accurate, uncertain, and inaccurate. (See Table I)

(1) The attribution of the title to Ṭūsī is certain (**C**: accurate attribution/missing)

(2) The attribution of the title to Ṭūsī is uncertain (uncertain attribution/missing)

(3) The attribution of the title to Ṭūsī is inaccurate (*inaccurate attribution/missing*)

Table I: Ṭūsī's works regarding the manuscripts and titles

Manuscript's attribution / The title's attribution to Ṭūsī	Available			Missing
	Accurate	**Uncertain**	**Inaccurate**	
Accurate	Accurate /accurate (A)	Accurate /uncertain (B)	*Accurate /inaccurate*	Accurate /missing (C)
Uncertain	Uncertain /accurate (D)	*Uncertain /uncertain*	*Uncertain /inaccurate*	*Uncertain /missing*
Inaccurate	*Inaccurate /accurate*	*Inaccurate /uncertain*	*Inaccurate /inaccurate*	*Inaccurate /missing*

Of the above 12 possible states, only four will apply to our list as per the following considerations. The states that do not apply are italicized.

Any answer we give to the three questions above—(i), (ii), and (iii)—will fall within one of these 12 states. In reply to these questions regarding any particular work, we did not make any judgments; instead, we relied on the views of experts, and when there are conflicting views, we pointed to the disagreement and then classified the attribution (of the title to Ṭūsī or the manuscript to the title) as an uncertain attribution. Therefore, there is no accurate attribution in our classification since in cases where the attribution of a title to Ṭūsī or a manuscript to the title is rejected by a scholar, the attribution is deemed uncertain given that there were opposing views.

If a title is attributed to Ṭūsī and has not called into question by any scholar, then we consider its attribution as accurate, even if evidence for its attribution seems inadequate (such as "Sharāʾiṭ dīn al-Imāmiyya"). It should be noted that since Ṭūsī has listed many of his own works in his *al-Fihrist*, there is little disagreement among scholars about his works. There are disagreements only about three titles.

In the fourth stage, we organized our list of Ṭūsī's works in terms of answers provided by the experts as to whether their manuscripts are available: available works and missing works.

Available works: works that satisfy both of the following conditions: (1) their titles are attributed to Ṭūsī in the above five groups of sources, and (2) there is at least an alleged manuscript attributed to that title.

One note: An alleged manuscript is what is claimed by Āqā Buzurg Ṭihrānī or researchers after him to exist or is mentioned in lists of manuscripts such as those of the Library of Ayatollah Marʿashī Najafī or *Fankha*.

Missing works: Any work that is not available.

In the fifth stage, there are differences in various manuscripts or sources. In these cases, we show the relevant difference between parentheses if possible, such as "al-Jabābira (al-Khayābira)," and if a work has different titles, we merge them into one title. Moreover, sometimes the publishers invented titles for a work, which cannot be found in the above sources. In such cases, we mention the work with the title used by the publisher.

Next, we began to classify the works under eight categories: theology (*kalām*), jurisprudence (*fiqh*), hadith, the science of assessing the reliability of hadith transmitters (*rijāl*), Quranic sciences, principles of jurisprudence (*uṣūl al-fiqh*), supplications, and other works. In each category, we begin by providing a list of available works, and then list the missing works. As appropriate, we define more specific subcategories for each category.

In our introduction of manuscripts of works, we rest content with one or two manuscripts, which are selected in accordance with the following two criteria: (1) the date of the manuscript; we try to introduce the earliest manuscript among the available manuscripts, and (2) accessibility; sometimes an early manuscript can be found in a personal library, which it is difficult for researchers to obtain. In these cases, we introduce an available manuscript in public libraries, such as the Library of Ayatollah Marʿashī Najafī.

Comparison of the Lists

Well-known bibliographies of Ṭūsī's works are as follows:

A comparison of the bibliographies

Well-known bibliographies of Ṭūsī's work are as follows:

1. *Al-Fihrist* by Ṭūsī. In this work, Ṭūsī mentions his own work, which is of utmost credibility. He only mentions forty-two works, which does not cover all of his writing.

2. *Rijāl* by al-Najāshī who was contemporary with Ṭūsī and, in fact his fellow in Mufīd's lectures. Al-Najāshī died ten years before Ṭūsī's death (in 450 AH/1058). For this reason, although his list includes few works by Ṭūsī, it is very reliable. He has listed nineteen works by Ṭūsī.

3. *Maʿālim al-ʿulamā'* by Ibn Shahrāshūb Māzandarānī. After the above two works, this is the oldest bibliography in which Ṭūsī's works are mentioned, although it is not of the same degree of reliability. Ibn Shahrāshūb mentions forty-seven works by Ṭūsī.

4. *Al-Dharīʿa* by Āqā Buzurg Ṭihrānī, which does not involve a unified list of Ṭūsī's works in one place.

5. *Aʿyān al-Shīʿa* by Muḥsin Amīn, which includes forty-six works by Ṭūsī.

6. *Fihristgān nusakh khaṭṭī Īrān (The list of Iranian manuscripts)*: it includes 37 manuscripts which are available in Iran. Thus, it is not a comprehensive list.

7. *Pazhūhishī pīrāmūn muṣannafāt Shaykh Ṭūsī (A research concerning Shaykh Ṭūsī's writings)* by Muḥammad Adībīmihr. It includes fifty titles, which is relatively comprehensive.

8. *Zindigīnāmi wa-āthār Shaykh Ṭūsī (Shaykh Ṭūsī's biography and bibliography)* by Āqā Buzurg Ṭihrānī, which includes forty-six titles.

The present bibliography compares with the above bibliographies in what follows:

1. Our bibliography includes fifty-three titles, the most comprehensive list, including all the lists mentioned in the above sources.

2. The present bibliography is the most recent so far, which includes writings that have gone unnoticed because of failure to take note of lists of manuscripts (including "Sharā'iṭ dīn al-Imāmiyya").

3. Titles that cannot certainly be taken as the same are mentioned separately, and so, it will be easier for researchers to find the title they are looking for.

4. To the extent possible, the views of scholars concerning the accuracy of the attribution of a title to Ṭūsī, or the accuracy of the attribution of a manuscript to a title, as well as the possible identification of the titles, are mentioned, which makes it easier to overview the disagreements.

5. When possible, in this bibliography, we sought to mention the order and time in which the works were written. This was only possible for some writings where there is evidence concerning the time of their writing.

The main references of the primary sources

(These are the main references cited here and in Part III of the book. That is, the bibliography of primary sources—the works of Ṭūsī. Their full bibliographical information is mentioned below.)

References

1. Ibn Shahrāshūb, Muḥammad ibn ʻAlī. 1380 AH. *Maʻālim al-ʻulamāʼ fī fihrist kutub al-Shīʻa wa-asmāʼ al-muṣannifīn minhum qadīmā wa-ḥadīthā: tatimma kitāb* al-Fihrist *li-l-Shaykh Abū Jaʻfar al-Ṭūsī (Prominent scholars concerning the bibliography of books of the Shia and the names of their authors both old and recent: a supplement to* Al-fihrist *by al-Shaykh Abū Jaʻfar al-Ṭūsī).* Najaf: Al-Maṭbaʻat al-Ḥaydariyya.
2. Ibn Ṭāwūs, ʻAlī ibn Mūsā. 1409 AH. *Fatḥ al-abwāb (Opening of the gates).* Beirut: Muʼassasa Āl al-Bayt li-Iḥyāʼ al-Turāth.
3. Adībīmihr, Muḥammad. 1384. "Pazhūhishī pīrāmūn muṣannafāt Shaykh Ṭūsī" (A research concerning Shaykh Ṭūsī's writings), *Pazhūhish Dīnī*. (12): 129-49.
4. Āqā Buzurg Ṭihrānī 1403 .AH *Al-Dharīʻa ila taṣānīf al-Shīʻa (The recourse to the writings of the Shia).* Beirut: Dar al-Adwa'.
5. ʻAlīriḍā Mīrzā Muḥammad and Sayyid Ḥamīd Ṭabībiyān. 1376 SH. *Zindigīnāmi wa-āthār Shaykh Ṭūsī) Biography and bibliography of Shaykh Ṭūsī(.* Tehran: Institute for Humanities and Cultural Studies.
6. Amīn, Muḥsin. 1403 AH. *Aʻyān al-Shīʻa (The prominent Shia).* Beirut: Dār al-Taʻāruf li-l-Maṭbūʻāt.
7. Anṣārī, Muḥammad Iqbāl. 1350 SH. *Shaykh al-Ṭāʼifa Abū Jaʻfar al-Ṭūsī wa-muʼallafātuh (Master of the Denomination Abū Jaʻfar al-Ṭūsī and his writings).* In *Al-Dhikrā al-alfiyya li-l-Shaykh al-Ṭūsī*

(The Thousandth Anniversary of Shaykh Ṭūsī). Mashhad: Ferdowsi University.

8. Dirāyatī, Muṣṭafā. 1390 SH. *Fihristgān nuskhi-hāyi khaṭṭī Iran (Fankhā) (List of Manuscripts in Iran)*. Tehran: The National Library and Archives of Iran.

9. Rasūlī Maḥallātī, Hāshim. 1348 SH. *Mu'allafāt chāpī wa-ghayr chāpī Shaykh Ṭūsī (Shaykh Ṭūsī's published and unpublished writings)*. In *Yādnāmi-yi Shaykh Ṭūsī (Festschrift of Shaykh Ṭūsī)*. Mashhad: Ferdowsi University.

10. Riḍādād ,'Illiyyi and Sayyid Kāẓim Ṭabāṭabā'ī. 1387 SH. "Gāhshumārī-yi ā̱sār-i Shaykh Ṭūsī) "Chronology of Shaykh Ṭūsī's works .(*Muṭāli'āt-i Islāmī (Islamic Studies)*. (80).

11. Rawḍātī, Sayyid Muḥammad 'Alī. 1354 SH. *Du risāli-yi kalāmī az Shaykh Ṭūsī (Two theological essays by Shaykh Ṭūsī)*. In *Yādnāmi-yi Shaykh Ṭūsī (Festschrift of Shaykh Ṭūsī)*. Vol. 3. Mashhad: Ferdowsi University.

12. Subḥānī, Ja'far. 1406 AH. "Taṭawwur al-fiqh al-Shī'ī fi l-qarnayn 4 wa 5" (The development of Shiite jurisprudence in 4th and 5th centuries AH). *Turāthunā (Our Heritage)*. Vol. 1. No. 3. 14-36.

13. Ṣabāḥī, Mahdī. 1413 AH. "Ta'līfāt ma'rūf wa-mawjūd Shaykh Mufīd" (Shaykh Mufīd's well-known and available writings). *Al-Maqālāt wa-l-murāsalāt: majmū'i maqālāt kungiri-yi Shaykh Mufīd (Essays and correspondences: collected papers of the Conference of Shaykh Mufīd)*. Qom: Millennium of Shaykh Mufīd. 7-150.

14. Ṭūsī, Muḥammad ibn Ḥasan. 1414 AH. *Al-Mufaṣṣiḥ fī imāma Amīr al-Mu'minīn (The clarification in the imamate of Amīr al-Mu'minīn)*. In *al-Rasā'il al-'ashr (The ten essays)*. Qom: Jāmi'i Mudarrisīn.

15. Ṭūsī, Muḥammad ibn Ḥasan. 1490 AH. *Al-Istibṣār fī-mā ikhtalaf min al-akhbār (The insight into disputed hadiths).* Tehran: Islāmiyya.

16. Ṭūsī, Muḥammad ibn Ḥasan. 1414 AH. *Al-Jumal wa-l-ʿuqūd (The sentences and nodes).* In *Al-Rasāʾil al-ʿashr (The ten essays).* Qom: Jāmiʿi Mudarrisīn.

17. Ṭūsī, Muḥammad ibn Ḥasan. 1414 AH. *Al-Rasāʾil al-ʿashr (The ten essays).* Qom: Jāmiʿi Mudarrisīn.

18. Ṭūsī, Muḥammad ibn Ḥasan. 1417 AH. *Al-Ghayba (The occultation).* Qom: Dār al-Maʿārif Islāmī.

19. Ṭūsī, Muḥammad ibn Ḥasan. 1414 AH. *Al-Farq bayn al-nabī wa-l-imām (The distinction between the prophet and the imam).* In *Al-Rasāʾil al-ʿashr (The ten essays).* Qom: Jāmiʿi Mudarrisīn.

20. Ṭūsī, Muḥammad ibn Ḥasan. n.d. *Al-Fihrist (The list).* Najaf: Maktabat al-Murtaḍawiyya.

21. Ṭūsī, Muḥammad ibn Ḥasan. 1387 AH. *Al-Mabsūṭ fī fiqh al-Imāmiyya (The detailed in Imami jurisprudence).* Third edition. Tehran: Murtaḍawī.

22. Ṭūsī, Muḥammad ibn Ḥasan. *Talkhīṣ al-shāfī fi l-imāma (Summary of the healing on imamate).* Qom: Muḥibbīn.

23. Ṭūsī, Muḥammad ibn Ḥasan. *Fihrist kutub al-Shīʿa wa-uṣūlihim wa-asmāʾ al-muṣannifīn wa-aṣḥāb al-uṣūl (List of the books and principles of the Shiʿa and the names of Shiite authors and holders of principles).* Qom: Maktabat al-Muḥaqqiq al-Ṭabāṭabāʾī.

24. Ṭūsī, Muḥammad ibn Ḥasan. *Mukhtaṣar fī ʿamal yawm wa-layla (The brief in acts of days and nights).* In *Al-Rasāʾil al-ʿashr (The ten essays).* Second edition. Qom: Jāmiʿi Mudarrisīn.

25. Ṭūsī, Muḥammad ibn Ḥasan. *Masā'il al-khilāf ma' al-kull fi l-fiqh (Disputed problems with all in jurisprudence)*. First edition. Qom: Jāmi'i Mudarrisīn.

26. Ṭūsī, Muḥammad ibn Ḥasan. *Muqaddima fi l-madkhal ilā 'ilm al-kalām (An introduction to the entry into the science of theology)*. In *Al-Rasā'il al-'ashr (The ten essays)*. Second edition. Qom: Jāmi'i Mudarrisīn.

27. Majlisī, Muḥammad Bāqir. 1403 AH. *Biḥār al-anwār (Seas of lights)*. Beirut: Dar Iḥyā' al-Turāth al-'Arabī.

28. Noor Institute. 1391 SH. *Fihrist kutub Shaykh Ṭūsī (List of Shaykh Ṭūsī's books)*. In *Majmū'i āthār Shaykh Ṭūsī (Collected works of Shaykh Ṭūsī)*. Qom: Noor Institute.

29. Najāshī, Aḥmad ibn 'Alī. 1365 SH. *Rijāl (Figures)*. Sixth edition. Qom: Jāmi'i Mudarrisīn.

30. Wa'iẓzādih Khurāsānī, Muḥammad. 1363 SH. *Risāla ḥawl ḥayāt al-Shaykh al-Ṭūsī (An essay concerning the life of Shaykh Ṭūsī)*. In *Al-Rasā'il al-'ashr (The ten essays)*. Qom: Jāmi'i Mudarrisīn.

❖

The Methodology for Secondary Sources on Ṭūsī

In the section on secondary sources, we aim to introduce research on Ṭūsī in the following languages: European languages (English, German, and French), Arabic, and Persian. In the section on European languages, we list all papers, books, and dissertations about Ṭūsī. In the Persian and Arabic sections, we list all relevant books and papers. All secondary sources are, just like the primary sources, classified under different categories. However, the categories here are not exactly similar to those of the primary sources since there are, for example, contemporary books or papers about Ṭūsī's political theory, whereas Ṭūsī has no explicit essays or books concerning political sciences.

Our method for collecting the books was through databases of libraries. In each language, we first consulted academic databases (including both books and journal articles) in that language. Then we consulted the catalogues of major libraries in the language in question to check the found items and sometimes add new sources. The publications of the World Conference of al-Shaykh al-Ṭūsī have particularly helped.

As to European languages as well as Arabic, we sought to introduce and classify all books and papers about Ṭūsī. However, since there are too many Persian papers and books about Ṭūsī, we needed to make a selection, trying to introduce and classify top academic journal articles (known in Iran as "scientific-research articles") and books mainly focused on Ṭūsī.

Our debt to online sources (Noor software in Persian and the WorldCat website in English, and the Almanzuma website in Arabic) is too great to be appreciated and cited throughout in the book. For this reason, we mention each of these online sources here:

1. University of Exeter (http://www.exeter.ac.uk/library)

2. Worldcat (https://www.worldcat.org)
3. Libraries of Indiana University Bloomington (https://libraries.indiana.edu)
4. The SOAS Library (https://www.soas.ac.uk/)
5. Library of the Dominican Institute for Oriental Studies (https://alkindi.ideo-cairo.org/)
6. University of Texas Libraries (http://utexas.summon.serialssolutions.com)
7. The University of Chicago Library (https://catalog.lib.uchicago.edu/vufind/)
8. Brill publishing house (https://referenceworks.brillonline.com/subjects)
9. Qatar University Library (http://library.qu.edu.qa/library/)
10. Al-Maktaba al-Shamila (https://al-maktaba.org)
11. Dar Almandumah (http://search.mandumah.com/)
12. McGill University Library (https://www.mcgill.ca/library/)
13. University and State Library of Saxony-Anhalt (ULB) (http://bibliothek.uni-halle.de/)
14. Sorbonne library (https://catalogue.bis-sorbonne.fr/)
15. University library of the Humboldt University of Berlin (https://www.ub.hu-berlin.de/)
16. LMU Munich University Library (https://opac.ub.uni-muenchen.de/)
17. NYU Digital Library Technology Services (http://dlib.nyu.edu/)
18. Proquest (https://search.proquest.com/)

19. Duke University Libraries (https://library.duke.edu/)
20. Noor Specialized Journals)https://www.noormags.ir/)
21. Iran Book and Literature House (db.ketab.ir)
22. Publications of the World Conference of al-Shaykh al Ṭūsī (https://www.noormags.ir/view/en/magazine/number/23211)

Table II: lists of Ṭūsī's works

	Title	Publication Information	Manuscript Availability	Manuscript Attribution	Title's Attribution to Ṭūsī
1	*Al-Farq bayn al-nabī wa-l-imām*	Publisher: Jāmiʿi Mudarrisīn Place: Qom Year: 1414 AH	Available	Accurate	Accurate
2	*Al-Ghayba*	Publisher: Dār al-Maʿārif Islāmī Place: Qom Year: 1411 AH	Available	Accurate	Accurate
3	*Al-Mufaṣṣiḥ fī l-imāma*	Publisher: Jāmiʿi Mudarrisīn Place: Qom Year: 1414 AH	Available	Accurate	Accurate
4	*Talkhīṣ al-shāfī fī l-imāma*	Publisher: Muḥibbīn Place: Qom Year: 1382 SH	Available	Accurate	Accurate
5	*Risāla fī l-iʿtiqādāt*	Publisher: Jāmiʿi Mudarrisīn Place: Qom Year: 1414 AH	Available	Accurate	Doubtful
6	*Masāʾil uṣūl al-dīn / Masāʾil al-Ṭūsī*	-	Available	Accurate	Accurate

	Title	Publication Information	Manuscript Availability	Manuscript Attribution	Title's Attribution to Ṭūsī
7	*Al-Iqtiṣād al-hādī ilā ṭarīq al-rashād*	Publisher: Dār al-Aḍwā' Place: Beirut Year: 1406 AH	Available	Accurate	Accurate
8	*Sharḥ mā yata'allaq bi-l-uṣūl min jumal al-'ilm wa-l-'amal*	Publisher: Rā'id Place: Qom Year: 1394 SH	Available	Accurate	Accurate
9	*Mukhtaṣar mā la-yasi' al-mukallaf al-ikhlāl bih*	-	Available	Doubtful	Accurate
10	*Al-Masā'il al-kalāmiyya*	Publisher: Jāmi'i Mudarrisīn Place: Qom Year: 1414 AH	Available	Accurate	Accurate
11	*Muqaddima fī l-madkhal ilā 'ilm al-kalām*	Publisher: Jāmi'i Mudarrisīn Place: Qom Year: 1414 AH	Available	Accurate	Doubtful
12	*Al-Kāfī*	-	Missing	-	Accurate
13	*Uṣūl al-'aqā'id*	-	Missing	-	Accurate
14	*Al-Istīfā' fī l-imāma*	-	Missing	-	Accurate
15	*Al-Masā'il al-Rāziyya fī l-wa'īd*	-	Missing	-	Accurate
16	*Mā yu'allal wa-mā lā-yu'allal*	-	Missing	-	Accurate
17	*Riyāḍat al-'uqūl*	-	Missing	-	Accurate

	Title	Publication Information	Manuscript Availability	Manuscript Attribution	Title's Attribution to Ṭūsī
18	*Al-Naqḍ 'alā Ibn Shādhān fī mas'alat al-ghār*	-	Missing	-	Accurate
19	*Al-Jumal wa-l-'uqūd fī l-'ibādāt*	Publisher: Dār al-Mufīd Place: Qom Year: 1413 AH	Available	Accurate	Accurate
20	*Al-Mabsūṭ fī fiqh al-Imāmiyya*	Publisher: Murtaḍawī Place: Tehran Year: 1387 AH	Available	Accurate	Accurate
21	*Al-Masā'il al-Ḥā'iriyya*	Publisher: Jāmi'i Mudarrisīn Place: Qom Year: 1414 AH	Available	Accurate	Accurate
22	*Al-Nihāya fī mujarrad al-fiqh wa-l-fatāwā*	Publisher: Dār al-Kitāb al-'Arabī Place: Beirut Year: 1400 AH	Available	Accurate	Accurate
23	*Masā'il al-khilāf ma' al-kull fī l-fiqh*	Publisher: Jāmi'i Mudarrisīn Place: Qom Year: 1407 AH	Available	Accurate	Accurate
24	*Al-Ījāz fī l-farā'iḍ*	Publisher: Jāmi'i Mudarrisīn Place: Qom Year: 1414 AH	Available	Accurate	Accurate
25	*Mas'ala fī taḥrīm al-fuqā'*	Publisher: Jāmi'i Mudarrisīn Place: Qom Year: 1414 AH	Available	Accurate	Accurate
26	*Mukhtaṣar fī 'amal yawm wa-layla*	Publisher: Jāmi'i Mudarrisīn	Available	Accurate	Accurate

	Title	Publication Information	Manuscript Availability	Manuscript Attribution	Title's Attribution to Ṭūsī
		Place: Qom Year: 1414 AH			
27	*Al-Masā'il al-Junbalā'iyya*	-	Missing	-	Accurate
28	*Al-Masā'il al-Ḥalabiyya*	-	Missing	-	Accurate
29	*Masā'il Ibn al-Barrāj*	-	Missing	-	Accurate
30	*Mas'ala fī mawāqīt al-ṣalāt*	-	Missing	-	Accurate
31	*Mas'ala fī wujūb al-jizya 'alā al-Yahūd wa-muntamīn ilā al-Jabābira (al-Khayābira)*	-	Missing	-	Accurate
32	*Manāsik al-ḥajj fī mujarrad al-'amal wa-l-ad'iya*	-	Missing	-	Accurate
33	*Al-Istibṣār fī-mā ikhtalaf min al-akhbār*	Publisher: Islāmiyya Place: Tehran Year: 1390 AH	Available	Accurate	Accurate
34	*Al-Majālis fī l-akhbār*	Publisher: Dār al-Thiqāfa Place: Qom Year: 1414 AH	Available	Accurate	Accurate
35	*Tahdhīb al-aḥkām*	Publisher: Islāmiyya Place: Tehran Year: 1365 SH	Available	Accurate	Accurate

	Title	Publication Information	Manuscript Availability	Manuscript Attribution	Title's Attribution to Ṭūsī
36	*Ikhtiyār al-rijāl*	Publisher: Markaz Nashr Āthār 'Allāma Muṣṭafawī Year: 1388 SH	Available	Accurate	Accurate
37	*Rijāl al-Ṭūsī*	Publisher: Jāmi'i Mudarrisīn Place: Qom Year: 1415 AH	Available	Accurate	Accurate
38	*Al-Fihrist*	Publisher: Fiqāhat Place: Qom Year: 1429AH	Available	Accurate	Accurate
39	*Al-Tibyān fī tafsīr al-Qur'ān*	Publisher: Dār Iḥyā' al-Turāth al-'Arabī Place: Beirut Year: -	Available	Accurate	Accurate
40	*Al-Masā'il al-rajabiyya fī tafsīr al-Qur'ān*	-	Missing	-	Accurate
41	*Al-Masā'il al-Dimashqiyya*	-	Missing	-	Accurate
42	*Al-'Udda fī uṣūl al-fiqh*	Publisher: Sitāri Place: Qom Year: 1417 AH	Available	Accurate	Accurate
43	*Sharḥ al-sharḥ fī l-uṣūl*	-	Missing	-	Accurate
44	*Mas'ala fī l-'amal bi-khabar al-wāḥid*	-	Missing	-	Accurate
45	*Mukhtaṣar al-miṣbāḥ / miṣbāḥ al-ṣaghīr*	Qom: Maktabat al-'Allāma al-Majlisī, 1435 AH	Available	Accurate	Doubtful

	Title	Publication Information	Manuscript Availability	Manuscript Attribution	Title's Attribution to Ṭūsī
46	*Miṣbāḥ al-mutahajjid fī 'amal al-sunna*	Publisher: Mu'assasa Fiqh al-Shi'a Place: Beirut Year: 1411 AH	Available	Accurate	Accurate
47	*Hidāyat al-mustarshid wa-baṣīrat al-muta'abbid*	-	Missing	-	Accurate
48	*Sharā'iṭ dīn al-Imāmiyya*	-	Available	Accurate	Accurate
49	*Al-Masā'il al-Qummiyya*	-	Missing	-	Accurate
50	*Uns al-waḥīd*	-	Missing	-	Accurate
51	*Mas'ala fī l-aḥwāl*	-	Missing	-	Accurate
52	*Al-Masā'il al-Ilyāsiyya*	-	Missing	-	Accurate
53	*Mukhtaṣar akhbār al-Mukhtār ibn Abī 'Ubayda (al-Thaqafī)*	-	Missing	-	Accurate
54	*Maqtal al-Ḥusayn 'alayh al-salām*	-	Missing	-	Accurate

Part One: Introduction

1.1. Ṭūsī: A Biography[1]

Muḥammad ibn Ḥasan al-Ṭūsī, known as "Shaykh al-Ṭā'ifa" (literally: head of the denomination) and "Shaykh Ṭūsī," was born in the month of Ramadan, 385 SH (September 995 AH). It is not known whether he was from the village "Ṭūs" near the city Ṭābarān or Nūghān, where the city of Mashhad in Iran is located today or from other villages in the vicinity of Ṭūs. But his title, "Ṭūsī," which appears in his own works and in the works of his contemporary scholar, Najāshī, implies that he was born in this area. At that time, most people living in Khorasan and the area of Ṭūs were Sunni Muslims, as were people in many other areas of Iran. However, there were families of Twelver Shiʿas living in Khorasan and areas adjacent to the mausoleum of the Eighth Shiite Imam al-Riḍā. People generally recognize them as Shiʿas, including the prominent Persian poet Ferdowsi (940-1019), who was contemporary with Shaykh Ṭūsī's teachers.

Ṭūsī learned the standard preliminary educational courses and was an educated student by his youth. At that time, Ṭūs, Neyshabur (or Nishapur), Sabzevar, Rey, and Qom were places where Ṭūsī could

1 This section is primarily a translated summary of the following sources: a. Āqā Buzurg Ṭihrānī ,Muḥammad Muḥsin. 1360 SH. *Zindigīnāmi-yi Shaykh Ṭūsī* [tra]. Translated by ʿAlīriḍā Mīrzāmuḥammad and Ḥamīd Ṭabībiyān. Tehran: Farhangistan Adab wa-Hunar; and b. Dawānī, ʿAlī. 1349 SH. *Hizāri Shaykh al-Ṭūsī*. Tehran: Dar al-Tabliqh Islami.

attend the courses of both Shiite and Sunni scholars, particularly Qom as the center of Shi'as, which was home to many scholars. It is not known, however, whether Ṭūsī stayed in Ṭūs during his youth or migrated to one of those cities. Arguably, Ṭūsī studied mainly in his birthplace with ordinary scholars, since he would mention eminent teachers in his works had he studied with them in any of those scholarly centers before the age of twenty-three.

In his younger years, on the one hand, Ghazni and Khorasan were ruled by the king Mahmud of Ghazni, who seriously propagated the Sunni denomination, and on the other hand, a major part of Iran was ruled by Shiite kings of the Buyid dynasty, including Rey, Fars, and Baghdad as centers of their government.

Four years before his birth, the head of Shiite scholars of hadith, Muḥammad ibn Bābway al-Qummī, known as Shaykh Ṣadūq, died in Rey in 381 AH/991 CE, and in the year of his birth, Ṣāḥib ibn 'Abbād, the eminent scholar and minister of Rukn al-Dawla Daylamī died (in 385 AH/991 CE). One year before his birth, Ferdowsi finished his long epic poem *Shahnama* in Ṭūs (384 SH/990 CE), and then in 401 AH/996 CE when Ṭūsī was still in Ṭūs, Ferdowsi edited and finalized *Shahnama* under the name of the king Mahmud of Ghazni in order to receive a great prize, though he did not receive a good prize because he was "Rāfiḍī" (a pejorative term to refer to Shi'as).

Ṭūsī spent his young years at a time when such events were talks of the town in Khorasan: the popularity of the Shiite poet Ferdowsi's epic poems in his hometown of Ṭūs, publication of intellectual and written work of the leader of Shiite scholars in Iran, Ibn Bābawayh, which amounted to three hundred books and essays, and was circulated in a large area from Bukhara to Baghdad, the news about the Shiite government of the Buyid dynasty, and anecdotes and writings of their prominent minister Ṣāḥib ibn 'Abbād, who was praised by four hundred competent poets. These must have played some role in the activities of the young intelligent Shiite student in Khorasan, Ṭūsī. Moreover, these enabled him to reach high stages of progress and high degrees of knowledge.

After Shaykh Ṣadūq's demise, Muḥammad ibn Muḥammad ibn Nuʿmān al-Baghdādī, known as Shaykh Mufīd, assumed the leadership of Shiʿas. Mufīd lived in the center of the caliphate and the great Islamic seminary in Baghdad. He had many prominent students. In 408 AH/1017 CE, when he was twenty-three, Ṭūsī migrated to Baghdad to attend the lectures of Mufīd and other prominent scholars.

At that time, Baghdad, as a glorious city and the center of the Abbasid caliphate, ruled a significant portion of the Islamic world: from the Red Sea and Mediterranean coasts to China's borders, except Andalusia and Northern Africa. From a scholarly point of view, the city was home to many scholars from all Islamic denominations.

Scholars of the four Sunni denominations (Ḥanafī, Mālikī, Shāfiʿī, and Ḥanbalī), along with prominent Imami and Zaydi Shiite scholars, discussed and debated freely over all sorts of issues, each trying to bring out the superiority of their own logic.

The famous scholar of the time in Baghdad was the Arab leader of Shiite scholars—a courageous speaker, intelligent, and an expert of all sciences of his time. Shiite and Sunni scholars admitted Mufīd's superiority.

Qāḍī ʿAbd al-Jabbār al-Muʿtazilī (d. 415 AH/1025 CE), the leader of Muʿtazilī Muslims, and Qāḍī Abū Bakr al-Bāqilānī (d. 403 AH/1013 CE), the leader of Ashʿarites, and ʿAlī ibn ʿĪsā al-Rummānī (d. 384 AH/994 CE), a well-known scholar of Arabic syntax and theology (*kalām*), were among those with whom Mufīd debated and defeated. The title, "Mufīd" (literally: useful), was given to him when he was young by ʿAlī ibn ʿĪsā al-Rummānī on account of his scholarly accomplishments.

Mufīd's contemporary, Ibn al-Nadīm, writes in 336 AH/947 CE or 338 AH/949 CE when Mufīd was just forty years old, that "Mufīd inherited the headship of Shiite theologians in our time. He is superior to everyone in the science of theology based on the Imami denomination. He is meticulous and quick on the trigger. I have met him; he is a master of all sciences... He is at the highest position in jurisprudence and theology" (*Fihrist Ibn Nadīm*, pp. 266-294)[2]. This quote captures how Mufīd was received at the time. Ṭūsī in his *al-Fihrist* and Dhahabī in his *Mīzān al-i'tidal* attribute nearly two hundred works to Mufīd. Mufīd's status and impact among both Shiite and Sunni Muslims was to such an extent that 'Aḍud al-Dawla Daylamī, the powerful Buyid king who ruled the Islamic world then and who manipulated the caliph in Baghdad, visited Mufīd in his house, particularly when Mufīd was sick (*Tārīkh Baghdād*, 3:231)[3].

Mufīd lived in Baghdad, engaged in handling the affairs of Shi'as and training students who were to become eminent Shiite scholars. Mifīd's best-known students were Sayyid Murtaḍā (d. 436 AH/1044 CE), his brother Sayyid Raḍī (406 AH/1015 CE) who collected *Nahj al-balāgha*, Abu-l-'Abbās Aḥmad ibn 'Alī al-Najāshī (460 AH/1058 CE), Ja'far ibn Muḥammad Dūrīstī (d. after late Dhu al-Hijjah 474 SH/May 1082 CE), Sālār ibn 'Abd al-'Azīz (d. 448 AH/1056 CE), Abu l-Fatḥ Karājakī (d. 449 AH/1057 CE), and Muḥammad ibn Ḥasan Ḥamza, known as Abū Ya'lā Ja'farī (d. after 436 AH/1044 CE). When Ṭūsī arrived in Baghdad and attended the courses of the old Mufīd, all these figures except Sayyid Raḍī were alive. Ṭūsī soon grabbed Mufīd's attention with his intelligence and hard work.

---

[2] Ibn al-Nadīm, Muḥammad b. Isḥāq. 1348 AH. *Al-Fihrist*. Cairo: Al-Maktabat al-Tijāriyyat al-Kubrā.

[3] Khaṭīb al-Baghdādī, Aḥmad b. 'Alī. 1349 AH/1931. *Tārīkh Baghdād* (History of Baghdad). Beirut: Maṭba'at al-Sa'āda.

Ṭūsī attended the lectures of Mufīd for five years; that is, until Mufīd's death. Moreover, he attended the lectures of other Shiite scholars, including Abu l-Ḥasan ʿAlī ibn Aḥmad ibn Abī Jayyid (d. after 408 AH/1017 CE), Aḥmad ibn Muḥammad ibn Mūsā, known as Ibn Ṣalt Ahwāzī (d. 409 AH/1018 CE), Ḥusayn ibn ʿUbaydullāh Ghaḍā'irī (d. 411 AH/1020 CE), and Aḥmad ibn ʿAbd al-Wāḥid, known as Ibn ʿAbdūn (d. 423 AH/103 CE). Ṭūsī mentions all his teachers in his books. He says that he studied twenty, out of two-hundred works by Mufīd, with Mufīd himself.

Before the age of twenty-eight, Ṭūsī wrote an exposition for Mufīd's *Al-Muqniʿa* (a short text on Shiite jurisprudence). He finished the section on cleanliness (*ṭahāra*) and the first part of the section on prayer (*ṣalāt*) before Mufīd's death in 413 AH/1022 CE). Ṭūsī's *Tahdhīb al-aḥkām*, which has been, and still is, one of the four reliable sources of Shiite jurisprudence in the last ten centuries, is a fruit of his young years.

After Mufīd's death, Ṭūsī attended the lectures of his successor Sayyid Murtaḍā for twenty-three years, particularly in theology, jurisprudence, and principles of jurisprudence. In the epilogue of his *Mustadrak al-wasā'il*, Mīrzā Ḥusayn Nūrī mentions thirty-seven people as Ṭūsī's teachers based on his works and ʿAllāma Ḥillī's permission to children of Zuhra. However, Ṭūsī only mentions five scholars as his teachers in his *Al-Fihrist*, *Tahdhīb*, *Istibṣār*, and other works: Mufīd, Ghaḍā'irī, Ibn ʿAbdūn, Ibn Abī Jayyid, and Ibn Ṣalt, but in his works of theology, jurisprudence, principles of jurisprudence, and Quranic exegesis, he often cites the words of his teacher Sayyid Murtaḍā. This can be found in his *Tibyān*, *ʿUddat al-uṣūl*, *Al-Ghayba*, and *Talkhīṣ al-shāfī*.

In his *Al-Fihrist*, Ṭūsī writes that Sayyid Murtaḍā was superior to everyone in theology, jurisprudence, principles of jurisprudence, literature, poetry, syntax, meanings of poems, philology, etc. Sayyid Murtaḍā's collection of poems consists of over twenty thousand verses.

Moreover, he wrote many replies to questions from different cities and countries (p. 55)[4].

Ṭūsī as an Iranian scholar among Sunni Arab people, assumed the leadership of the Shiʿa after Mufīd and Murtaḍā. Sayyid Murtaḍā gave salaries to his students in proportion to their scholarly degrees. Ṭūsī received a monthly salary of twelve thousand dinars, and Qāḍī Ibn Barrāj received eight thousand dinars. Sayyid Murtaḍā passed away at eighty in 426 AH/1044 CE. He was the head of Shiʿas for twenty-three years. Although some of his prominent widely respected students such as Abū ʿAlī Jaʿfarī, Najāshī, and Karājakī were still alive, Ṭūsī remained unrivaled in assuming the Shiite leadership. At this time, Ṭūsī was fifty-one years old. In virtue of his scholarly career, social status, and his mastery of religious doctrines and denominations, Ṭūsī was awarded the chair of theology by the caliph of the time, al-Qāʾim bi-Amr Allāh. He sat on the chair and gave lectures in theology and religious doctrines. This position, as well as leadership of the Shiite community in Baghdad, seem to have been held by Ṭūsī due to his moderate character.

For twelve years after Sayyid Murtaḍā, Ṭūsī held the Shiite leadership in Baghdad. His leadership was accepted by Shiʿas in Iraq, Iran, and the Levant. However, the presence of an Iranian Shiite scholar in the center of a Sunni Arab world was not tolerated by some people, particularly in that Mufīd and Sayyid Murtaḍā were both native Arabs from Baghdad. As evidenced by well-known Sunni books of history, such as *al-Muntaẓam* by Ibn Jawzī (d. 597 AH/1201 CE), *al-Kāmil* by Ibn Athīr (d. 630 AH/1233 CE), *al-Bidāya wa-l-nihāya* by Ibn Kathīr Shāmī (d. 774 AH/1373 CE), and *Lisān al-mīzān* by Ibn Ḥajar al-ʿAsqalānī (d. 852 AH/1449 CE), since Ṭūsī's arrival in Baghdad (in 408 AH/1017 CE) until 448 AH/1056 CE when Ṭūsī was compelled to leave

[4] Shaykh al-Ṭūsī, Muḥammad b. al-Ḥasan. 1356 AH. *Al-Fihrist*. Najaf: n.p.

Baghdad, unfortunate events took place for Shiʿas in Karkh neighborhood, which left a deep impact on their circumstances and Ṭūsī's fate. According to the above sources, in 408 AH/1017 CE, Muharram of 417 SH (February 1026 CE), 430 AH/1038 CE, 432 AH/1040 CE, the Day of Ashura in 440 SH (June 25, 1048 AH), Safar of 443 SH (June 1051 CE), and 445 AH/1053 CE, bloody events occurred in the course of which many people were murdered and injured, and the houses, shops, and possessions of many Shiʿas were plundered. Some of these took place during the lifetime of Mufīd, some took place during the leadership of Sayyid Murtaḍā, and the rest under Ṭūsī. The unrest was controlled during the periods of Mufīd and Sayyid Murtaḍā because Shiite Daylamite kings hindered the rebels. After Sayyid Murtaḍā's death, the rebels were diminished by the interventions of tribe leaders and the caliph himself. But in 447 AH/1055 CE and 448 AH/1056 CE, the crisis became more profound, and all people of Baghdad collectively rebelled against the Shiʿas, which discouraged Ṭūsī from staying in Baghdad and convinced him to migrate. Here is the story in a nutshell. Shiite Buyid kings had influence over Abbasid caliphs for over a century, which led the caliph al-Qāʾim bi-Amr Allāh to encourage the Seljuk ruler Tughril Beg—a fanatic Sunni Muslim—to occupy Baghdad and put an end to the Buyid rule and prevent Basāsīrī from accomplishing his goals. The Turkish slave-soldier Basāsīrī invited people to obey the Fatimid rulers of Egypt, which endangered the Abbasid caliphate. Tughril Beg arrived in Baghdad in 447 AH/1055 CE and saved the Abbasid caliph. Basāsīrī fled Baghdad, and the Buyid dynasty came to an end. Since then, Shiʿas experienced increasing pressures, since both the government and people were freed from the Buyid dominance and seized the opportunity to oppress Shiite scholars who had been influential in the last twenty-five years.

After Tughril Beg arrived in Baghdad, Shiʿas of Karkh neighborhood were prohibited from citing *ḥayy ʿalā khayr al-ʿamal* (literally: haste to the best act) and were ordered to cite the Sunni alternative of *al-ṣalāt khayr min al-nawm* (literally: prayer is better than sleep). Moreover, Shiite mottos and graffiti, such as *Muḥammad and ʿAlī khayr al-bashar* (literally: Muhammad and ʿAlī are best people) were erased from the walls of Karkh neighborhood. A Shiite cloth-dealer in Karkh was murdered and hung. Then Ṭūsī escaped to a hiding place, and his house was looted. In Safar 449 CE (April 1057 AH), Ṭūsī's books were set on fire in public in front of the Naṣr Mosque.

Ṭūsī had escaped to Najaf probably in 447 AH/1055 CE, but his house was looted two years later in 449 AH/1057 CE. His migration to Najaf was timely since, in the next year, when Basāsīrī gained more power and governed Baghdad in the absence of Tughril Beg, the Shiʿas found an occasion for revenge. But Tughril Beg soon returned to Baghdad, Basāsīrī fled and was then killed, and Baghdad was occupied by proponents of the Abbasid caliphate, at which point many houses in the neighborhood of Karkh were set on fire, including the library of Shāhpūr ibn Ardashīr—Bahāʾ al-Dawla Daylamī's Shiite minister. The library was founded in 381 AH/991 CE in the Karkh neighborhood to be used by Shiite scholars. It contained the most precious books of the time, including ten thousand and four hundred books transcribed from books available in Iran, Rome, China, India, and Iraq. It also contained one hundred precious copies of the Qurʾan with the handwritings of children of Ibn Muqla—the well-known Arab calligrapher. Most of these books were burned down by opponents, some were looted, and some were stolen by ʿAmīd al-Mulk.

The mausoleum of the first Shiite Imam ʿAlī ibn Abī Ṭālib, located in Najaf, made it the best destination for Ṭūsī. At that time, Najaf was not a city or even a village. Only a few pilgrims and Shiʿas lived near the mausoleum. Najaf flourished during Daylamite kings who frequently visited the mausoleum. However, when Ṭūsī moved to Najaf, it was not as thriving as it was during the Buyid and Daylamite dynasties. Ṭūsī spent the last twelve years of his life in Najaf, which undoubtedly attracted many of his students to the place, and as a result, many Shiʿas migrated to Najaf. Arguably, Ṭūsī was the founder of the Shiite Seminary of Najaf, which is still home to many scholars and students.

Ṭūsī had a son called Ḥusayn, known as Abū ʿAlī Ṭūsī, who inherited the Shiite authority from his father. Abū ʿAlī received permission from his father in 455 AH/1063 CE; that is, fifty years before his father's death. As it seems, he always accompanied his father both in Baghdad and in Najaf and learned all Islamic sciences from him. He was arguably a competent scholar of jurisprudence and hadiths. Abū ʿAlī Ṭūsī had a son called Abū Naṣr Muḥammad ibn Ḥasan. According to Āqā Buzurg Ṭihrānī, it is surprising that no information is available about him, although he was a Shiite authority just like his father and his grandfather. Ṭūsī had two daughters as well, both of whom studied Islamic sciences. One of them is the grandmother of the well-known scholar Muḥammad ibn Idrīs Ḥillī, the author of *Sarā'ir al-aḥkām*, and the other was the wife of the scholar Muḥammad ibn Aḥmad ibn Shahriyār, the guardian of the shrine of Imam ʿAlī.

Ṭūsī's teachers

According to Mīrzā Ḥusayn Nūrī, Ṭūsī had thirty-seven teachers in hadiths (in his *Mustadrak wasā'il al-Shīʿa*, 3:509)[5]. Nūrī has extracted their names from Ṭūsī's own writings as well as ʿAllāma Ḥillī's *al-Ijāzat al-kabīra*. Having said that, the teachers often mentioned by Ṭūsī in his *Al-Fihrist*, *Al-Tahdhīb*, and *Al-Istibṣār* are five figures:

1. Shaykh Abū ʿAbd Allāh Aḥmad ibn ʿAbd al-Wāḥid ibn Aḥmad al-Bazzāz, known as Ibn Ḥāshir Murra or Ibn ʿAbdūn Ukhrā (d. 423 AH/1031 CE).
2. Shaykh Aḥmad ibn Muḥammad ibn Mūsā, known as Ibn Ṣalt al-Ahwāzī (d. after 408 AH/1017 CE).

[5] Nūrī, Mīrzā Ḥusayn. 1321 AH. *Mustadrak al-wasā'il wa-mustanbaṭ al-masā'il*. Tehran: n.p.

3. Shaykh Abū ʿAbd Allāh Ḥusayn ibn ʿUbayd Allāh ibn Ghaḍāʾirī (d. 411 AH/1020 CE).

4. Shaykh Abu l-Ḥusayn ʿAlī ibn Aḥmad ibn Muḥammad ibn Abī Jayyid (d. after 408 AH/1017 CE).

5. Abū ʿAbd Allāh Muḥammad ibn Muḥammad ibn Nuʿmān, known as Shaykh Mufīd (d. 413 AH/1022 CE).

These are the teachers from whom Ṭūsī often transmitted hadiths. Other masters from whom Ṭūsī transmitted hadiths are as follows:

1. Abu l-Ḥusayn Ṣaffār (or ibn al-Ṣaffār).

2. Abu l-Ḥusayn ibn Sawār al-Maghribī. In his *al-Ijāzat al-kabīra,* ʿAllāma Ḥillī mentions him as a Sunni teacher of Ṭūsī.

3. Shaykh Abū Ṭālib ibn Gharūr.

4. Qāḍī Abū Ṭayyib Ṭabarī Ḥuwayrī (d. after 408 AH/1017 CE).

5. Abū ʿAbd Allāh Akhū Sarwa.

6. Abū ʿAbd Allāh ibn Fārsī.

7. Abū ʿAlī ibn Shādhān the theologian. In his *al-Ijāzat al-kabīra,* ʿAllāma Ḥillī mentions him as a Sunni teacher of Ṭūsī.

8. Abū Manṣūr al-Sukrī. According to Afandī in his *Riyāḍ,* he was probably Sunni or Zaydi, but according to Mīrzā Ḥusayn Nūrī, it is improbable that he was a Sunni on account of certain hadiths that he has transmitted. Still, no evidence counts against the possibility of him being Zaydi.

9. Aḥmad ibn Ibrāhīm al-Qazwīnī (d. after 408 AH/1017 CE).

10. Abu l-Ḥusayn or Abu l-ʿAbbās Aḥmad ibn ʿAlī al-Najāshī, the author of the well-known book *Rijāl* (d. 450 AH/1058 CE).

11. Jaʿfar ibn Ḥusayn ibn Ḥaska al-Qummī (d. after 408 AH/1017 CE).

12. Sharīf Abū Muḥammad Ḥasan ibn Qāsim al-Muḥammadī (d. after 408 AH/1017 CE).

13. Abū ʿAlī Ḥasan ibn Muḥammad ibn Ismāʿīl ibn Muḥammad ibn Ashnās, known as Ibn Ḥammāmī al-Bazzāz. He is mentioned by Sayyid ibn Ṭāwūs in his *al-Iqbāl* and by al-Ḥurr al-ʿĀmilī in his *Ithbāt al-hudāt*.

14. Abū Muḥammad Ḥasan ibn Muḥammad ibn Yaḥyā ibn Dāwūd al-Faḥḥām, known as Ibn Faḥḥām al-Sāmarrāʾī (d. after 408 AH/1017 CE).

15. Abu l-Ḥusayn Ḥasanbash al-Muqrī (d. after 408 AH/1017 CE).

16. Abū ʿAbd Allāh Ḥusayn ibn Ibrāhīm al-Qazwīnī (d. after 408 AH/1017 CE).

17. Abū ʿAbd Allāh Ḥusayn ibn Ibrāhīm ibn ʿAlī al-Qummī, known as Ibn Khayyāṭ.

18. Ḥusayn ibn Abī Muḥammad Hārūn ibn Mūsā Talluʿukbarī (d. after 408 AH/1017 CE).

19. Abū Muḥammad ʿAbd al-Ḥamīd ibn Muḥammad al-Muqrī al-Nīshābūrī.

20. Abū ʿAmr ʿAbd al-Waḥid ibn Muḥammad ibn ʿAbd Allāh ibn Muḥammad ibn Mahdī (d. after 410 AH/1019 CE).

21. Abu l-Ḥasan ʿAlī ibn Aḥmad ibn ʿUmar ibn Ḥafṣ al-Muqrī, known as Ibn Ḥammāmī al-Muqrī (d. after 408 AH/1017 CE). He is distinct from Ibn Ashnās who is also known as Ibn Ḥammāmī.

22. Sayyid Murtaḍā ʿAlam al-Hudā Abu l-Qāsim ʿAlī ibn Ḥusayn ibn Mūsā ibn Muḥammad ibn Ibrāhīm ibn Imam Mūsā al-Kāẓim (d. 436 AH/1044 CE).

23. Abu l-Qāsim ʿAlī ibn Shibl ibn Asad al-Wakīl (d. after 410 AH/1019 CE).

24. Qāḍī Abu l-Qāsim ʿAlī al-Tanūkhī, the son of Qāḍī Abū ʿAlī Muḥsin, the son of Qāḍī Abu l-Qāsim ʿAlī ibn Muḥammad ibn Abi-l-Fahm Dāwūd ibn Ibrāhīm ibn Tamīm al-Qaḥṭānī. He was a student and companion of Sayyid Murtaḍā. In his *al-Ijāzat al-kabīra*, ʿAllāma Ḥillī refers to him as a Sunni teacher of Ṭūsī, but according to *Riyāḍ*, he was arguably Shiite.
25. Abu l-Ḥusayn ʿAlī ibn Muḥammad ibn ʿAbd Allāh Bushrān, known as Ibn Bushrān al-Muʿaddil (d. after 411 AH/1020 CE).
26. Muḥammad ibn Aḥmad ibn Abi l-Fawāris al-Ḥāfiẓ (d. after 411 AH/1020 CE).
27. Abū Zakariyyā Muḥammad ibn Sulaymān al-Ḥarrānī (or Ḥamdānī). He was from Ṭūs, and probably was a teacher of Ṭūsī before the latter migrated to Iraq.
28. Muḥammad ibn Sinān. In his *al-Ijāzat al-kabīra*, ʿAllāma Ḥillī refers to him as a Sunni teacher of Ṭūsī.
29. Abū ʿAbd Allāh Muḥammad ibn ʿAlī ibn Ḥimawī al-Baṣrī (d. after 413 AH/1022 CE).
30. Muḥammad ibn ʿAlī ibn Khashīsh ibn Naḍr ibn Jaʿfar ibn Ibrāhīm al-Tamīmī (d. after 408 AH/1017 CE).
31. Abu l-Ḥasan Muḥammad ibn Muḥammad ibn Muḥammad ibn Mukhallad (d. after 417 AH/1026 CE).
32. Sayyid Abu l-Fatḥ Hilāl ibn Muḥammad ibn Jaʿfar al-Ḥaffār (b. 322AH/933CE, d. 414 AH/1023 CE).

These thirty-two figures plus those five scholars—amounting to thirty-seven people—were Ṭūsī's teachers as can be derived from his work and other sources. It goes without saying that in his *Mustadrak*, Nūrī refers to thirty-eight teachers of Ṭūsī, but this is because he repeats Ḥasan ibn Muḥammad ibn Ismāʿīl ibn al-Ashnās once more under Ḥasan ibn Ismāʿīl. The above names come from Nūrī's *Mustadrak*.

Ṭūsī's students

Ṭūsī had over three hundred students, including many Sunni students, as pointed out by Majlisī in his *Biḥār al-anwār*, Shushtarī in his *al-Maqābis*, Khwānsārī in his *al-Rawḍāt*, and Mudarris in his *al-Rayḥāna*, among others. Many of these students are still unknown to the extent that even Shaykh Muntajab al-Dīn ibn Bābawayh (d. after 585 AH/1189 CE), who was close to Ṭūsī's period, could not identify many of them, and in his *al-Fihrist*, he only mentions twenty-six students of Ṭūsī, and Sayyid Mahdī Baḥr al-ʿUlūm in his *al-Fawāʾid al-rijāliyya*, added four other names to the list, although Mīrzā Ḥusayn Nūrī does not mention them.

Here is a list of Ṭūsī's students (note that descriptions, such as "reliable jurist," come from the above sources):

1. Ādam ibn Yūnus ibn Abi-l-Muhājir al-Nasīfī ,a reliable righteous jurist.
2. Abū Bakr Aḥmad ibn Ḥusayn ibn Aḥmad Khuzāʿī Nīshābūrī, a reliable precious author and scholar.
3. Abū Ṭālib Isḥāq ibn Muḥammad ibn Ḥasan ibn Ḥusayn ibn Muḥammad ibn ʿAlī ibn Ḥusayn ibn Bābawayh Qummī, a reliable scholar.
4. Abū Ibrāhīm Ismāʿīl, a reliable scholar and Abū Ṭālib Isḥāq's brother.
5. Abu l-Khayr Baraka ibn Muḥammad ibn Baraka Asadī, a reliable scholar.
6. Abu l-Ṣalāḥ Taqī ibn Najm al-Dīn Ḥalabī, a reliable scholar and great author.
7. Sayyid Abū Ibrāhīm Jaʿfar ibn ʿAlī ibn Jaʿfar Ḥusaynī, a reliable scholar of hadiths.

8. Shaykh Shams al-Islām Ḥasan ibn Ḥusayn ibn Bābawayh al-Qummī, known as Ḥaska, an author and leader.
9. Shaykh Abū Muḥammad Ḥasan ibn ʿAbd al-ʿAzīz ibn Ḥasan Jubhānī (or Juhbānī), a reliable jurist.
10. Abū ʿAlī Ḥasan ibn Muḥammad ibn Ḥasan Ṭūsī, a reliable great scholar and Ṭūsī's own son.
11. Muwaffaq al-Dīn Ḥusayn ibn Fatḥ Wāʿiẓ Jurjānī, a reliable scholar and leading jurist.
12. Imām Muḥyi-l-Dīn Abū ʿAbd Allāh Ḥusayn ibn Muẓaffar ibn ʿAlī ibn Ḥusayn Ḥamdānī, a reliable scholar of great reputation. He lived in Qazvin, Iran.
13. Sayyid ʿImād al-Dīn Abu l-Ṣamṣām or Abu l-Waḍḍāḥ Dhu l-Faqār ibn Muḥammad ibn Miʿbad Ḥusaynī Marwzī.
14. Abū Muḥammad Zayd ibn ʿAlī ibn Ḥusayn Ḥusaynī (or Ḥasanī), a sayyid (a descendant of Prophet Muhammad) and jurist.
15. Sayyid Zayn ibn Dāʿī Ḥusaynī ,a knowledgeable scholar.
16. Shaykh Saʿd al-Dīn ibn Barrāj, a well-known jurist.
17. Shaykh Abu l-Ḥasan Sulaymān ibn Ḥasan ibn Salmān Ṣahrashtī, a reliable jurist.
18. Shaykh Shahrāshūb Sarawī Māzandarānī, a great scholar of hadiths and the grandfather of Muḥammad ibn ʿAlī, the author of *Maʿālim al-ʿulamāʾ*.
19. Shaykh Ṣāʿid ibn Rubayʿa ibn Abī Ghānim, a reliable jurist.
20. Shaykh ʿAbd al-Jabbār ibn ʿAbd Allāh ibn ʿAlī Muqrī Rāzī, known as Mufīd.
21. Shaykh Abū ʿAbd Allāh ʿAbd al-Raḥmān ibn Aḥmad Ḥusayn Khuzāʿī Nīshābūrī, known as Mufīd.

22. Shaykh Muwaffaq al-Dīn Abu l-Qāsim ʿUbayd Allāh ibn Ḥasan ibn Ḥusayn ibn Bābawayh, a reliable jurist.

23. Shaykh ʿAlī ibn ʿAbd al-Ṣamad Tamīmī Sabzawārī, a reliable jurist.

24. Ghāzī ibn Aḥmad ibn Abī Manṣūr Sāmānī, a learned ruler and ascetic jurist.

25. Kurdī ibn ʿIkbir ibn Kurdī Fārsī, a reliable scholar and righteous jurist who lived in Aleppo.

26. Imām Shaykh Jamāl al-Dīn Muḥammad ibn Abi-l-Qāsim Ṭabarī Āmulī.

27. Abū ʿAbd Allāh Muḥammad ibn Aḥmad ibn Shahriyār Khāzin Gharawī, a trusted scholar and righteous jurist.

28. Shaykh Muḥammad ibn Ḥasan ibn ʿAlī Fattāl, a learned scholar and author of *Rawḍat al-wāʿiẓīn*.

29. Shaykh Abu l-Ṣalt Muḥammad ibn ʿAbd al-Qādir ibn Muḥammad, a righteous jurist.

30. Abu l-Fatḥ Muḥammad ibn ʿAlī Karāchakī, a reliable scholar, a learned author, and a Shiite jurist.

31. Shaykh Abū Jaʿfar Muḥammad ibn ʿAlī ibn Ḥasan Ḥalabī.

32. Shaykh Abū ʿAbd Allāh Muḥammad ibn Hibat Allāh Ṭirāblusī, a reliable jurist from Tripoli.

33. Ṣadr al-Ashrāf Sayyid Murtaḍā Abu l-Ḥasan Muṭahhar ibn Abi-l-Qāsim ʿAlī ibn Abi-l-Faḍl Muḥammad Ḥusaynī Dībājī, a religious leader of his time.

34. Sayyid Muntahā ibn Abī Zayd ibn Kabābakī Ḥusaynī Jurjānī, a jurist.

35. Dhu-l-Maʿālī Zayn al-Kufāt Abū Saʿīd Manṣūr ibn Ḥusayn Ābī, a learned jurist.

36. Abū Ibrāhīm Nāṣir ibn Riḍā ibn Muḥammad ibn ʻAbd Allāh ʻAlawī Ḥusaynī, a reliable jurist and scholar of hadiths, and a sayyid (that is, a descendent of Prophet Muḥammad).

These thirty-six scholars were students of Ṭūsī. Ṭihrānī casts doubts about the students added by Sayyid Mahdī Baḥr al-ʻUlūm and Shaykh Asad Allāh Dizfūlī. He argues that Shaykh ʻUbayd Allāh ibn Ḥasan might not have been a student of Ṭūsī, since his son, Shaykh Muntajab al-Dīn, does not mention his father among Ṭūsī's students in his *al-Fihrist*. Ṭihrānī also argues that Karāchakī (d. 449 AH/1057 CE) and Jamāl al-Dīn Muḥammad Ṭabarī might not have been Ṭūsī's students, since if the latter is the same as ʻImād al-Dīn Muḥammad ibn Abi-l-Qāsim ʻAlī Ṭabarī Āmulī, then he must have been a student of Abū ʻAlī, Ṭūsī's son, since he transmits most of his hadiths from people who lived after 500 AH/1106 CE.

Ṭūsī taught and wrote in Najaf for twelve years until his death on Sunday, Muharram 22, 460 SH (December 2, 1067 AH) seventy-five. He was buried by his students Shaykh Ḥasan ibn Mahdī Salīqī, Shaykh Abū Muḥammad Ḥasan ibn ʻAbd al-Wāḥid ʻAyn Zarbī, and Shaykh Abu l-Ḥasan Lu'lu'ī, and in compliance with his own will, he was buried in his own house in Najaf. According to his will, his house was changed into a mosque after his death, and people visited his mausoleum. This is a well-known mosque in Najaf in which many great scholars taught for centuries. The mosque is located in the Mishrāq neighborhood in Najaf and is adjacent to Imam ʻAlī's shrine to its north. The gate of the shrine leading to the mosque is called "Bāb al-Ṭūsī" (Ṭūsī gate). The mosque was rebuilt twice after its first construction.

❖

1.2. The Impact of Shaykh al-Ṭūsī on Development of Rapprochement Efforts

Melanie G. Raza

Muḥammad b. al-Ḥasan b. ʿAlī b. al-Ḥasan, well known as Shaykh al-Ṭūsī (d. 460 AH/ 1067 CE) was a renowned Twelver Shiʿi scholar during the 10th - 11th centuries. Although he was born in Tus (385 AH/995 CE), he migrated to what is modern day Baghdad (408 AH). This afforded al-Ṭūsī the opportunity to study under Shaykh al-Mufīd (d. 413 AH/1022 CE) for five years. Al-Ṭūsī was known to have upwards of 37 teachers, including Sharīf al-Murtaḍā (d. 436 AH/1044 CE), and he taught more than 300 students himself, from various ideologies, including both Sunni and Shiʿi. When his house and the library of Shapur were burned down in Baghdad, al-Ṭūsī was forced to move to Najaf, which became a tremendous turning point in Shiʿi scholarship. He contributed to a completely new era of Islamic literacy and learning, which served as the foundation for the Islamic Seminary of Najaf. As such, he was honored with the title Shaykh al-Ṭāʾifa, translated as "the master of the Shiʿa."[6]

Al-Ṭūsī wrote works on numerous disciplines such as theology, jurisprudence, Quranic exegesis, hadith, and supplications. His ideas would become preliminary for scholars of religion, philosophy, and jurisprudence for future generations of scholars across different disciplines. Additionally, his insights and contributions would become the foreground for rapprochement efforts between Sunni and Shiʿi groups. Al-Ṭūsī's ideology can be applied to many contemporary issues in the current socio-political sphere.

---

[6] Amir-Moezzi, Mohammad Ali, "al-Ṭūsī", in: *Encyclopaedia of Islam, Second Edition,* edited by: P. Bearman, Th. Bianquis, C.E. Bosworth, E. van Donzel, W.P. Heinrichs. <http://dx.doi.org/10.1163/1573-3912_islam_SIM_7653>

In the Shiʿi world, perhaps al-Ṭūsī is best known for authoring two out of the four main Shiʿi texts of jurisprudential hadiths—*Al-Istibṣār* and *Tahdhīb al-aḥkām*—in addition to other major Shiʿi sources. Both of these texts are compilations of hadiths concerning the law or legal rulings. *Al-Istibṣār* contains approximately 5,500 hadiths while *Tahdhīb al-aḥkām* contains 13,600.[7]

Al-Ṭūsī was an integral part of the development of works on *uṣūl al fiqh* (principles of jurisprudence).[8] When analyzing the hadith literature, it is necessary to note that al-Ṭūsī did not adhere to two principles that are common tools used in *uṣūl al fiqh* today: 1) analogy (*qiyās*) and 2) independent reasoning (*ijtihād*). This signifies that the narrations in his collections were not swayed by shifting ideas or applications of analogy or consensus. Al-Ṭūsī's ideology of rational traditionalism indicates to today's society of scholars that the hadiths compiled in his book have undergone an intellectual process. In other words, his text is refined in that it is not committed to the *Akhbārī*s' method of pure traditionalism.[9] Thus, al-Ṭūsī should be credited with a greater level of reliability.

Al-Ṭūsī's reputation is such that, without his contributions, the Shiʿi legal school of thought would not exist. Al-Ṭūsī was a prolific scholar and writer, as he produced many other works, especially in response to other schools of thought. In particular, al-Ṭūsī's *Al-Khilāf fī l-Aḥkām*—translated as *Disagreements in Rulings*—known more widely as *Al-Khilāf*, "The Disagreements," has inspired generations of further

[7] Toussi, Seyyed Khalil. "Epistemic value of transmitted reports (hadiths) in Shi'ism." 2022. https://www.syncsci.com/journal/IJAH/article/view/IJAH.2021.01.004

[8] Tusi, Abu Ja'far Muhammad Ibn al-Hasan (1996). al-'Udda fi Usul al-Fiqh, ed. Ansari Qumi. Qum: M. R. Setareh.

[9] Abisaab, R. (2015). Shiʿi Jurisprudence, Sunnism, and The Traditionist Thought (Akhbārī) of Muhammad Amin Astarabadi (D. 1626-27). *International Journal of Middle East Studies, 47*(1), 5-23. doi:10.1017/S0020743814001421

scholarship even centuries after his demise.[10] Al-Ṭūsī completed this work in a total of six volumes, each of which was focused on specific topics and debates in Islamic jurisprudence. For example, the first volume was centered on topics, including the legal rulings for menstruation, purity, performing prayer, prayers for specific occasions such as eclipses, the rights of the dead, etc. *Al-Khilāf* was organized so the reader would approach the appropriate book by the index and seek his answer and opposing arguments all within the same section. It was produced for Shiʿas as well as individuals from other jurisprudential schools of thought. This was a monumental achievement for scholars, philosophers, and debaters of Islamic disciplines, as al-Ṭūsī had produced the first comparative intra-Muslim work.

Additionally, al-Ṭūsī authored another influential text known as *al-Mabṣūṭ*, a book of 70 chapters that discussed different principles of Islamic jurisprudence in great detail. These two texts had a profound impact on al-Ṭūsī's society, and its noticeable influence on rapprochement and fluid dialogue between adherents of different belief systems is incontestable:

> The former rector of al-Azhar, the revered Shaykh Abdul-Majeed Saleem, has been quoted as saying that he very much admired Shiʿitc fiqh after someone had given him a copy of the book titled Al-Mabsoot by Shaykh al-Tusi as a gift. He liked the book so much that he made statements saying that he reviewed this book prior to issuing any fatwa, binding religious edict; so, whenever he found in this book what convinced him that it was the best viewpoint, he adopted it without any hesitation, an open-mindedness which has now become so rare...[11]

---

[10] Al-Sadr, Muhammad Baqir. *Principles of Islamic Jurisprudence*. 2005.

[11] Al-Jibouri, Yasin T. "A Tribute to Sheikh Al-Tusi." https://www.al-islam.org/articles/tribute-sheikh-al-tusi-yasin-t-al-jibouri

The content of *Al-Khilāf* improved the legal discussions of scholarly debates as well as individuals who were seeking to learn Shiʿi beliefs. Unfortunately, a text such as *Al-Khilāf* that has the potential to contribute so much to the sectarian world today by providing methods of reckoning and reconciliation has largely been untouched and untranslated into the English language.

Interestingly, al-Ṭūsī's purpose in writing *Al-Khilāf* was to provide a means of dialogue between Sunni and Shiʿi scholars. Al-Ṭūsī was greatly influenced by his contemporary scholars to embark on this text. In the preface of *Al-Khilāf*, al-Ṭūsī noted that his fellow scholars requested him to respond to disputed issues among opposing schools of thought.[12] These scholars of other Islamic traditions wanted to be aware of the logic that their counterparts used to justify their opposing beliefs. In fact, the format and structure of *Al-Khilāf* was such that for every topic of discussion that al-Ṭūsī introduced, he framed the issue as a question ("*mas'ala*"), and beneath the *mas'ala*, he responded with his own thought-out and detailed answer ("*dalīlunā*" - literally translated as "our reasoning").[13] The first-person plural form represented by "*dalīlunā,*" signifies that al-Ṭūsī was representing the Shiʿi community of scholars and believers as a whole. With this being said, *Al-Khilāf* took the shape of a handbook for common believers as well as scholars wishing to engage in theological debates and exchanges with their Sunni and Shiʿi peers, largely taken from al-Ṭūsī's own scholarly encounters.[14]

---

[12] Al-Ṭūsī, Al-Khilāf fī l-Aḥkām.

[13] Ibid.

[14] Ansari, Hassan, and Sabine Schmidtke. 2014. Al-Shaykh al-Ṭūsī: His Writings on Theology and their Reception. In Daftary, Farhad and Gurdofarid Miskinzoda, ed. 2014. The study of Shi'i Islam: history, theology and law. London and New York: I.B. Tauris, New York: Palgrave Macmillan.

In *Al-Khilāf*, al-Ṭūsī discusses Twelver Shiʿi views as well as other religious schools of thought. What differentiated al-Ṭūsī from his contemporaries was that he mentioned the beliefs of different schools of Islamic jurisprudence alongside his own.[15] He also possessed the scholarly ability and was well-versed in other Islamic traditions to offer respectable and well-informed criticisms. He logically countered his opponents' beliefs and justified Twelver Shiʿi positions. Al-Ṭūsī relied heavily on the process of deductive reasoning, offering his own opinions by using the intellect and methods of analysis.[16] By basing his arguments and beliefs in logic, deductive reasoning, and the traditions transmitted from the Prophet, al-Ṭūsī successfully faced the challenge brought on by his contemporary scholars that are still relevant today.

Unlike other scholars, al-Ṭūsī was able to recognize his own bias, and he was also able to understand Sunni and Shiʿi legal rulings from their respective religious denominational viewpoints well enough to discuss them fluidly. This was not only present in al-Ṭūsī's writings, but also in his role as a teacher:

> Students and seekers of knowledge went in hordes to the residence of Shaykh al-Tusi in order to learn from him, so his house in Baghdad embraced seekers of knowledge whose number was estimated to be no less than three hundred renown mujtahids from among the Shiʿa faith in addition to countless Sunnis who attracted them with his own method and convincing style, presenting his evidence and treating everyone with the most lofty of Islamic ethical standards.[17]

[15] Al-Ṭūsī, Al-Khilāf fī l-Aḥkām.

[16] Ibid.

[17] Al-Jibouri, Yasin T. "A Tribute to Sheikh Al-Tusi." https://www.al-islam.org/articles/tribute-sheikh-al-tusi-yasin-t-al-jibouri

In this excerpt, it is conspicuous that al-Ṭūsī was a role model for students across many different backgrounds and beliefs. He drew students from Shiʿi as well as Sunni backgrounds, and he did not limit himself as simply a scholar on one belief tradition. Al-Ṭūsī achieved his purpose for writing *al-Khilāf*, but he also put into practice his teachings. In his writings and his role as a teacher, he successfully provided sound and significant arguments for Shiʿi beliefs based in the teachings and traditions of the Prophet.

Across all of his teachings and texts, al-Ṭūsī relied heavily on rationalism and implementing the intellect. He adopted this approach to Quranic and hadith studies. Furthermore, al-Ṭūsī shattered the boundaries of sectarian discourse by relying on scholarly opinions non-inclusive to the Shiʿi school of thought. In his commentary on the Qur'ān, *Al-Tibyān fī tafsīr al-Qur'ān*, al-Ṭūsī discusses the opinions of both Sunni and Shiʿi scholars before making his own deductions.[18] This type of scholarship proposed new methods for understanding the Qur'ān as well as hadith literature and opened the door to further understanding across different ideological groups.[19]

❖

[18] Tusi, Abu Ja'far Muhammad Ibn al-Hasan (1957-63). *al-Tibyan fi Tafsir al-Qur'an*, ed. Ahmad Shawqi al-Amin and Ahmad Habib Qasir al-'Amili . Najaf.

[19] Baghalian, Hossein. 2021. "Introducing Shaykh Tusi's hermeneutic perspective in interpreting the revelation words and predicates with an emphasis on al-tibyan fi tafsir al-Quran". *International Journal of Multicultural and Multireligious Understanding*, Vol. 8, Iss. 4: 233-247.

1.3. Chronology of Ṭūsī's Works

Tahdhīb al-aḥkām	408-448 AH (1017-1056)
Al-Nihāya	Probably around 415-435
Al-Istibṣār	After Tahdhīb and al-Nihāya
Al-'Udda	circa 432AH (1040) - after 436AH (1044)
Al-Istīfā' fi l-imāma	Before 436AH (1044)
Al-Mufaṣṣiḥ fi l-imāma	Before 437AH (1045)
Talkhīṣ al-shāfī	Finished in 432AH (1040)
Al-Fihrist	Before 436AH (1044) - after 436AH (1044)
Rijāl	Before 436AH (1044)
Al-Masā'il al-Rāziyya	Before 436AH (1044)
Sharḥ jumal al-'ilm	After 436AH (1044) - before 450AH (1058)
Al-Jumal wa-l-'uqūd	Before the completion of al-Mabsūṭ
Al-Ījāz fi l-farā'iḍ	Before the completion of al-Mabsūṭ
Al-Khilāf	After Tahdhīb and al-Istibṣār and before the completion of al-Mabsūṭ
Al-Mabsūṭ	Writing began probably a short time before the completion of al-Khilāf

Al-Tibyān	After 436AH (1044) - before 448AH (1056)
Mā yuʿallal wa-mā lā-yuʿallal	During al-Najāshī's lifetime
Mā lā-yasaʿ al-mukallaf	Before 450AH (1058)
Al-Muqaddima fi l-madkhal	Finished in 444AH (1052)
Riyāḍat al-ʿuqūl	Circa 445AH (1053) - 450AH (1058)
Mas'ala fi l-aḥwāl	Before 450AH (1058)
Mas'ala fi l-ʿamal bi-khabar al-wāḥid	Before 450AH (1058)
Mukhtaṣar fī ʿamal yawm wa-layla	Probably before Miṣbāḥ or around 430-436
Miṣbāḥ al-mutahajjid	Before 448AH (1056)
Al-Iqtiṣād	Probably before al-Ghayba
Al-Ghayba	Partly written in 447AH (1055)
Hidāyat al-mustarshid	Probably after 450AH (1058)
Ikhtiyār maʿrifat al-rijāl	456AH (1063)
Al-Amālī	Started before 448AH (1056) - a major part finished in 458AH (1065)
Mukhtaṣar akhbār al-Mukhtār	After 450AH (1058)
Al-Naqḍ ʿalā Ibn Shādhān	After 451AH (1059)

Manāsik al-ḥajj	After 452AH (1060)
Kitāb uns al-waḥīd	After 453AH (1061)
Maqtal al-Ḥusayn	After 454AH (1062)
Sharḥ al-sharḥ	Unfinished at the time of Ṭūsī's death (460AH/1067)

❖

1.4. Chronology of Ṭūsī's Life

385AH/995	Birth – Death of Ṣāḥib ibn ʿAbbād the Daylamite minister
408AH/1017	Migration to Baghdad – Attending Shaykh Mufīd's courses
413AH/1022	Shaykh Mufīd's death – Leadership of Sayyid Murtaḍā – Rebels and slaughters in Baghdad in Muharram
417AH/1026	Rebels and slaughters in Baghdad
430AH/1038	Rebels and slaughters in Baghdad
432AH/1040	Rebels and slaughters in Baghdad
436AH/1044	Sayyid Murtaḍā's death – Leadership of Ṭūsī
440AH/1048	Rebels and slaughters in Baghdad
443AH/1051	Rebels and slaughters in Baghdad
445AH/1053	Rebels and slaughters in Baghdad
447AH/1055	Tughril Beg's arrival in Baghdad and the end of the Buyid dynasty in Baghdad
448AH/1056	Migration from Baghdad to Najaf
449AH/1057	House plundered and his books burned in Baghdad
460AH/1067	Death

❖

1.5. Ṭūsī in classical bibliographies

1. *Fihrist kutub al-Shīʿa wa-uṣūlihim wa-asmāʾ al-muṣannifīn wa-aṣḥāb al-uṣūl (List of the books and principles of the Shiʿa and the names of Shiite authors and holders of principles)*, p. 447.

2. Ṭūsī, Muḥammad ibn Ḥasan, vol. 1, Maktabat al-Muḥaqqiq al-Ṭabāṭabāʾī, Qom, Iran, first edition, 1420 AH.

3. *Kashf al-ẓunūn ʿan asāmi l-kutub wa-l-funūn (Removing suspicions from the names of books and arts)*, vol. 1, p. 452.

4. Ḥājī Khalīfa, Muṣṭafā ibn ʿAbd Allāh, two volumes, Dār Iḥyāʾ al-Turāth al-ʿArabī, Beirut, Lebanon, first edition.

5. *Kashf al-ḥujub wa-l-astār ʿan asmāʾ al-kutub wa-l-asfār (Removing the veils and covers from the names of books and writings)*, p. 31.

6. Kantūrī, Iʿjāz Ḥusayn ibn Muḥammad Qulī, one volume, Library of Ayatollah Marʿashī Najafī, Qom, Iran, second edition, 1409 AH.

7. 4. *Rijāl al-Najāshī (Najāshī's figures of hadiths)*, p. 403.

8. Najāshī, Aḥmad ibn ʿAlī, one volume, Jāmiʿi Mudarrisīn, Qom, Iran, sixth edition, 1365 SH.

9. *Maʿālim al-ʿulamāʾ fī fihrist kutub al-Shīʿa wa-asmāʾ al-muṣannifīn minhum qadīmā wa-ḥadīthā: tatimma kitāb* al-Fihrist *li-l-Shaykh Abī Jaʿfar al-Ṭūsī (Prominent scholars, a list of Shiite books and the names of their early and recent authors: a supplement to Abū Jaʿfar al-Ṭūsī's* al-Fihrist*)*, p. 114.

10. Ibn Shahrāshūb, Muḥammad ibn ʿAlī, one volume, al-Matbaʿat al-Haydariyya, Najaf, Iraq, first edition, 1380 AH.

11. *Al-Durr al-thamīn fī asmāʾ al-muṣannifīn (The precious pearl about the names of authors)*, p. 158.

12. Ibn al-Sā'ī ,'Alī ibn Anjab, one volume, Dār al-Gharb al-Islāmī, Tunisia, first edition, 1430 AH.

13. *Rijāl al-'Allāma al-Ḥillī ('Allāma Ḥillī's figures of hadiths)*, p. 148.

14. 'Allāma Ḥillī, Ḥasan ibn Yūsuf, one volume, Al-Sharīf al-Raḍī, Qom, Iran, second edition, 1402 AH.

15. *Shadharāt al-dhahab fī akhbār man dhahab (Nuggets of gold about the news of those who have passed away)*, vol. 6, p. 207.

16. Ibn 'Imād, 'Abd al-Ḥayy ibn Aḥmad, 11 volumes, Dār Ibn Kathīr, Damascus, Syria, first edition, 1406 AH.

Part Two: Bibliography of Biography

2.1. Ṭūsī in classical ṭabaqāt

1. *Ṭabaqāt al-Shāfiʿiyya al-kubrā (The great Shāfiʿī generations(*, vol. 4, p. 126.

   Subkī, ʿAbd al-Wahhāb ibn ʿAlī, ten volumes, Dār Iḥyāʾ al-Kutub al-ʿArabiyya, Cairo, Egypt, first edition.

2. *Manāqib al-Imām al-Shāfiʿī wa-ṭabaqāt aṣḥābih (Virtues of Imam Shāfiʿī and generations of his companions)*, p. 431.

   Ibn Qāḍī Shuhba, Abū Bakr ibn Aḥmad, one volume, Dār al-Bashāʾir, Damascus, Syria, first edition, 1424 AH.

3. *Ṭabaqāt al-mufassirīn (Generations of Quranic exegetes)*, p. 80.

   Suyūṭī, ʿAbd al-Raḥmān ibn Abī Bakr, one volume, Dār al-Kutub al-ʿIlmiyya, Manshūrāt Muḥammad ʿAlī Bayḍūn, Beirut, Lebanon, first edition.

4. *Ṭabaqāt al-mufassirīn (Generations of Quranic exegetes)*, vol. 2, p. 130.

   Dāwūdī, Muḥammad ibn ʿAlī, two volumes, Dār al-Kutub al-ʿIlmiyya, Manshūrāt Muḥammad ʿAlī Bayḍūn, Beirut, Lebanon, first edition.

5. *Ṭabaqāt al-mufassirīn (Generations of Quranic exegetes)*, p. 124.

   Adina Wī, Aḥmad ibn Muḥammad, one volume, Maktabat al-ʿUlūm wa-l-Ḥikam, Medina, Saudi Arabia, first edition, 1417 AH.

6. *Ṭabaqāt a'lām al-Shī'a (Generations of prominent Shias)*, vol. 2, p. 161.

7. Āqā Buzurg Ṭihrānī ,Muḥammad ibn Ḥasan ibn 'Alī ibn Ḥasan, seventeen volumes, Dār Iḥyā' al-Turāth al-'Arabī, Beirut, Lebanon, one volume, 1430 AH. *Mu'jam rijāl al-ḥadīth wa-tafṣīl ṭabaqāt al-ruwāt (Encyclopedia of hadith figures and elaboration of generations of hadith transmitters)*, vol. 16, p. 257. Khū'ī, Abu l-Qāsim, twenty-four volumes, [no publisher], [no place], fifth edition, 1413AH.

❖

2.2. Modern studies (1980-2020)

Books

1. Haydari Malikmian, Firiydun. 1391 SH. *Shaykh Tusi*. Tehran: *Mu'assisi-yi Farhangi Madrisi-yi Burhan.*

2. Kumpani Zari', Mahdi. 1392 SH. *Tusi-pazhuhi (majmu'i maqalati dar barrisi-yi ara', ahwal wa-athar Shaykh Tusi)* [tra]. Tehran: Khani Kitab.

3. Kumpani Zari', Mahdi. 1395 SH. *Shaykh Tusi pishwa-yi 'aliman shi'i* [tra]. Tehran: Waya.

Encyclopedia and dictionary entries

1. Amir-Moezzi, Mohammad Ali. *Encyclopaedia of Islam*, 2nd ed., s.v. "al-Ṭūsī". Published online, 2012.

Dissertations and theses

1. Ramyar, Mahmud. 1977. *Shaykh Tusi: the life and works of a Shiite leader*. Doctoral diss. University of Edinburgh.

Part Three: Bibliography of primary sources

3.1. Kalām

3.1.1. Prophethood

1. Al-Farq bayn al-nabī wa-l-imām (A)

"The distinction between the prophet and the Imam" is a concise essay about the distinction between prophets and Imams, how prophethood is distinguished from imamate, and what "prophet" and "imam" mean. It contains brief arguments, deferring further elaboration to the author's *Kitāb al-imāma* and *al-Masā'il al-Ḥalabiyya* (Ṭūsī 1414 AH, "Al-Farq bayn al-nabī wa-l-imām," 114). Ṭūsī mentions this work in his own *al-Fihrist* (p. 161). The essay has been published in six pages.

The essay is listed in the following classical bibliographies: Ṭūsī's *al-Fihrist* (n.d., 161), Ibn Shahrāshūb's *Ma'ālim al-'ulamā'* (1380 AH, 115), Āqā Buzurg Ṭihrānī's *al-Dharī'a* (1403 AH, 20:362).

A manuscript of the work is available in Malik Library in Tehran (manuscript no. 1626/12). The scribe is unknown, and the date of writing is 854 AH/1450 CE).

The essay has been critically edited and published in a collection of Ṭūsī's works under *al-Rasā'il al-'ashr (The ten essays)* by Jāmi'i Mudarrisīn in Qom in 1414 AH (1993 CE).

3.1.2. Imamate

2. Al-Ghayba (A)

"The occultation" is a book by Ṭūsī concerning the Twelfth Shiite Imam al-Mahdī. Ṭūsī mentions this work in his own *al-Fihrist* (n.d., 161). It is also known as "Al-Ghayba li-l-ḥujja" (The occultation of the proof) and "al-Ḥujja" (The proof). It consists of eight chapters in which various issues are discussed concerning Imam al-Mahdī, from his birth, proofs for his existence, miracles, and occultation. Ṭūsī wrote the work at the request of a prominent scholar (*al-Ghayba*, 1411 AH, 2). As the author makes it explicit, part of the work was written in 447 AH (1055 CE) (see Ṭūsī, 1411 AH, 112, 358) when Ṭūsī lived in Baghdad. The book has been published in 479 pages.

It has been listed in the following classical bibliographies: Ṭūsī's *al-Fihrist* (n.d., 161), Ibn Shahrāshūb's *Maʿālim al-ʿUlamāʾ* (1380AH, 115), and Āqā Buzurg Ṭihrānī in his *al-Dharīʿa* (1403 AH, 16:79).

Manuscripts of the book are available in Markaz Iḥyāʾ in Qom, Iran (manuscript number: 3764) and in the Library of Majlis in Tehran, Iran (manuscript number: 18404/9).

The book has been critically edited and published by Dār al-Maʿārif Islāmī in Qom in 1411 AH (1990 CE).

3. Al-Mufaṣṣiḥ fi l-imāma (A)

"The clarification on imamate" is a work by Ṭūsī mentioned by him in his own *al-Fihrist* (n.d., 160), Najāshī (1365 SH, 403), and Ibn Shahrāshūb (1380 AH, 115). The essay was written at the request of an eminent scholar, who some people believe was Qāḍī Ibn Barrāj (Subḥānī 1406 AH, 25). It is a brief essay concerning imamate, not structured into parts and sections. In this work, Ṭūsī briefly deals with arguments for the imamate of Imām ʿAlī and the Twelve Imams. The essay was published in twenty-two pages within *al-Rasā'il al-ʿashr*. It was written during the lifetime of Sayyid Murtaḍā (Wāʿiẓzāda 1363 SH, 30). Some people believe that it was written before *Talkhīṣ al-shāfī* (Rasūlī Maḥallātī 1348 SH, 1:273; Anṣārī 1350 SH, 2:517). However, some people have objected to this view, holding that the two works were written at the same time (Riḍādād and Ṭabāṭabā'ī 1387 SH, 59-60).

The essay is mentioned in the following classical bibliographies: Ṭūsī's *al-Fihrist* (n.d., 16), Najāshī's *Rijāl* (1365 AH, 403), Ibn Shahrāshūb's *Maʿālim al-ʿulamā'* (1380AH, 115), and Āqā Buzurg Ṭihrānī's *al-Dharīʿa* (1403 AH, 21:369).

A manuscript of the essay is available in the Center for the Great Islamic Encyclopedia in Tehran, Iran (manuscript number: 2155/2). Its scribe is not known, but it was transcribed in twenty-two pages in the thirteenth century AH (nineteenth century CE). Another manuscript is available in the Library of Ayatollah Marʿashī Najafī in Qom, Iran (manuscript number: 12806/3). It was written by Muḥammad Amīn ibn Yaḥyā Khū'ī (Ṣadr al-Islām) in 1334 AH (1915 CE).

The essay was critically edited and published in *al-Rasā'il al-ʿashr (The ten essays)* by Jāmiʿi Mudarrisīn in Qom in 1414 AH.

4. Talkhīṣ al-shāfī fi l-imāma (A)

"Summary of the healer on imamate" is a work by Ṭūsī mentioned by him in his own *al-Fihrist* (n.d., 160), by Najāshī (1365 SH, 403), and by Ibn Shahrāshūb (1380 AH, 114). It consists of excerpts from Sayyid Murtaḍā's *al-Shāfī fi l-imāma (The healer on imamate)* along with additions. The work was finished in 432 AH (1040 CE), four years before Sayyid Murtaḍā's death (Ṭūsī, *Talkhīṣ al-shāfī fi l-imāma* 1382 SH, 4:227). Some people have presented evidence for the view that

Ṭūsī began writing this book after he had started to write his *al-'Udda* (Riḍādād and Ṭabāṭabā'ī 1387 SH, 60). Since *al-Shāfī* was not a coherent, consistent work in that it included Sayyid Murtaḍā's replies to objections by Qāḍī 'Abd al-Jabbār in his *Mughnī*, and contained many repetitions, Ṭūsī decided to eliminate repetitive materials and reorganized the book in a new structure (Ṭūsī, *Talkhīṣ al-shāfī fi l-imāma* 1382 SH, 1:52).

This theological book deals with diverse issues about imamate. It has been published in four volumes in 1071 pages.

The book is mentioned in the following classical bibliographies: Ṭūsī's *al-Fihrist* (n.d., 160), Ibn Shahrāshūb's *Ma'ālim al-'ulamā'* (1380 AH, 114), Najāshī's *Rijāl* (1365 SH, 403), and Āqā Buzurg Ṭihrānī's *al-Dharī'a* (1403 AH, 4:423).

A manuscript of the book is available in Sipahsālār Library in Tehran, Iran (line 2282, registration no. 1323). The manuscript is transcribed from the one written, edited, annotated, and taught by 'Allāma Majlisī (d. 1110 AH/1699 CE). Majlisī's commentaries are also transcribed in this manuscript.

Another manuscript of the book is available in the Library of Theology and Islamic Doctrines (manuscript number: 867) in 237 pages. It was written by 'Abd Allāh ibn Qāsim 'Alī. The writing of the manuscript began on Safar 24, 1234 (December 23, 1818) and was finished on Jumada al-Thani 3. 1235 AH (March 18th, 1820 CE). Online link of the manuscript: http://manuscript.um.ac.ir/moreinfo-1668-pg-1.html.

Another manuscript is available in the Library of Ayatollah Mar'ashī Najafī (manuscript number: 3199). It was written by 'Abd al-Karīm ibn Muḥammad Ṣādiq Abharī Jiyyī Iṣfahānī in 268 pages. The writing was finished on Thursday, Rajab 26, 1091 (August 22, 1680). The manuscript was compared and edited in 1097 AH (1686 CE).

The book was critically edited and published in four volumes by Muḥibbīn Publications in Qom, Iran, in 1382 SH.

3.1.3. Miscellaneous

5. Risāla fi l-iʿtiqādāt (D)

"An essay on beliefs" is a theological essay, which is not mentioned in any bibliographies or biographies of Ṭūsī. Āqā Buzurg Ṭihrānī introduces several manuscripts under "Muqaddimat al-kalām" (Introduction to theology) or "Muqaddima fi l-madkhal ilā 'ilm al-kalām" (Introduction to the entry into the science of theology) and speculates that "Risāla fi l-iʿtiqādāt" might be part of "Muqaddimat al-kalām" (Ṭihrānī 1402 AH, 22:92; 1376 SH, 60-3). A number of scholars have argued, however, that some of these manuscripts belong to another theological essay by Ṭūsī, which is not mentioned in biographies and bibliographies, and is edited and published as "Risāla fi l-iʿtiqādāt" (Rawḍātī 1354 SH, 710-2).

The essay includes twenty-five arguments concerning monotheism, prophethood, and imamate. It was published in six pages within *al-Rasā'il al-ʿashr* (Ṭūsī 1414 AH).

Three manuscripts of the essay are available in the Central Library of the University of Tehran: first, manuscript number: 712:8, which is written in the eleventh century AH (seventeenth century CE). Second, manuscript number 1810:10 written by Sulṭān Maḥmūd ibn ʿAlī Ṭabasī in the eleventh century AH (seventeenth century CE). And third, manuscript number 3108 written by Aḥmad ibn Ḥusayn Raḍawī in 1274 AH (1858 CE).

The essay was critically edited and published in *al-Rasā'il al-ʿashr* by Jāmiʿi Mudarrisīn in Qom in 1414 AH.

6. Masāʾil uṣūl al-dīn (A)

"Problems of the principles of religion" is not attributed to Ṭūsī in any of his bibliographies or biographies. Wāʿiẓzāda Khurāsānī attributes the essay to Ṭūsī based on two manuscripts available in Astan Quds Razavi in Mashhad, Iran (Wāʿiẓzāda 1363 SH, 44). Other researchers, too, have provided evidence supporting the claim (Adībīmihr 1384 SH, 143). It is also known as "Thalāthūn masʾala" (Thirty problems) and "Masāʾil al-Ṭūsī" (Problems of Ṭūsī) (Adībīmihr 1384 SH, 142). It is noteworthy that there are two works mentioned in Āqā Buzurg Ṭihrānī's *al-Dharīʿa* under "Al-Masāʾil al-Ṭūsiyya" (Ṭūsī problems), one of which is written by Sayyid Murtaḍā and the other by Khwāja Naṣīr al-Dīn Ṭūsī (Ṭihrānī 1403 AH, 20:356), but neither of these is relevant to this essay. The essay has not yet been published. Since the manuscripts were not available to us, we could not find further information here.

7. Al-Iqtiṣād al-hādī ilā ṭarīq al-rashād (A)

"The guiding moderation in the way of rectitude" is mentioned by Ṭūsī in his *al-Fihrist* as "al-Iqtiṣād al-hādī ilā ṭarīq al-rashād" (n.d., 161), by Ibn Shahrāshūb as "Majmūʿ al-iqtiṣād fī-mā yajib ʿalā al-ʿibād" (1380 AH, 115), and by Āqā Buzurg Ṭihrānī in his *al-Dharīʿa* as "al-Iqtiṣād al-hādī ilā ṭarīq al-rashād" (1403 AH, 2:269). This is an elaborate book including an introduction and six sections concerning religious beliefs and worships. The first five sections that constitute the bulk of this work are devoted to religious beliefs—monotheism, justice, divine promise (*waʿd*) and threat (*waʿīd*), prophethood, and imamate. The final section includes jurisprudential issues about prayer, zakat, fasting, hajj, and jihad.

Given that, in this work, Ṭūsī defers issues of Imam Mahdī's occultation to his *Talkhīṣ al-shāfī*, rather than his *al-Ghayba*, it has been speculated that he wrote *al-Iqtiṣād* before *al-Ghayba* (Riḍādād and Ṭabāṭabā'ī 1387 SH, 66). The book was published in 446 pages.

The book is mentioned in the following classical bibliographies: Ṭūsī's *al-Fihrist* (n.d., 161), Ibn Shahrāshūb's *Ma'ālim al-'ulamā'* (1380 AH, 115), and Āqā Buzurg Ṭihrānī's *al-Dharī'a* (1403 AH, 2:269).

A manuscript of the book is available in Library of Majlis in Tehran, Iran (manuscript number: 10120/7). It was written in 255 pages by 'Alī ibn Muḥammad ibn Ḥasan Khurāsānī in 1036 AH (1626 CE). The manuscript was owned by Muḥammad Bāqir ibn Shaykh Asad Allāh. Another manuscript is available in the library of the University of Tehran (manuscript number: F-2969). This was written by 'Abd al-Majīd ibn Muẓaffar ibn Ḥasan ibn Muḥammad ibn Maḥrūm al-Tūblī al-Kūrī on Thursday, Jumada al-Awwal 24, 1044 AH (November 15, 1634 CE).

The book was critically edited and published by Dār al-Aḍwā' in Beirut, Lebanon, in 1406 AH.

8. Sharḥ mā yata'allaq bi-l-uṣūl min jumal al-'ilm wa-l-'amal (A)

"Exposition of what belongs to principles in *Jumal al-'ilm wa-l-'amal*" is mentioned by Ṭūsī in his own *al-Fihrist* (n.d., 161). Given the content of the book, Najāshī has called it "Tamhīd al-uṣūl" (Prolegomenon to the principles) (Najāshī 1365 SH, 403; Ṭihrānī 1403 AH, 4:433). It is also known as "Sharḥ jumal al-'ilm wa-l-'amal" (Adībīmihr 1384SH, 137).

This is an exposition of, and commentary on, the theological part of Sayyid Murtaḍā's *Jumal al-'ilm wa-l-'amal (Statements of knowledge and practice)*. It is structured into four sections, each of which contains a number of chapters. It begins with discussing the nature of obligatory acts, arguing that knowledge of God is the primary obligation. This is followed by issues such as incipience (*ḥudūth*) of physical objects, their features, God's existence and attributes, obligation, divine promise (*wa'd*) and threat (*wa'īd*), enjoining the right and forbidding the wrong, prophethood, and imamate. The book is published in 630 pages.

It was written after the death of Sayyid Murtaḍā in 436 AH (1044 CE) (Wā'iẓzāda 1363, 31) and before Najāshī's death (since he lists the book in his *Rijāl*); that is, before 450 AH (1058 CE).

The book is mentioned in the following classical bibliographies: Ṭūsī's *al-Fihrist* (n.d., 161), Najāshī's *Rijāl* (1365 SH, 403), and Āqā Buzurg Ṭihrānī's *al-Dharī'a* (1403 AH, 4:433).

A manuscript of the book is available in Astan Quds Razavi in Mashhad, Iran (manuscript number: 54). It is written in 227 pages, but the scribe is not known, and it has missing parts. Another manuscript of the book is available in the library of the University of Tehran (manuscript number: 6627/2). It is written by Abu l-Qāsim Ḥusaynī, but the date of writing is not known.

The book was critically edited by 'Abd al-Raḥīm Sulaymānī Bihbahānī and published by Rā'id in Qom, Iran, in 1394 SH.

9. Mukhtaṣar mā lā-yasa' al-mukallaf al-ikhlāl bih (B)

"Summary of what the duty-bound person cannot breach" is an essay by Ṭūsī. Ṭūsī himself mentions it in his *al-Fihrist* with the above title (n.d., 160). Najāshī mentions it as "Mā lā-yasa' al-mukallaf al-ikhlāl bih" (1365 SH, 403), and Ibn Shahrāshūb as "Mā lā-yasa' al-mukallaf tarkuh" (What the duty-bound person cannot omit) (1380 AH, 115). It has been claimed that the essay is concerned with theology (Āqā Buzurg Ṭihrānī 1376 SH, 53; Amīn 1403 AH, 9:166), but some people have doubts over whether it is a theological or jurisprudential work

(Wāʿiẓzāda 1363 SH, 42). Since Najāshī has mentioned the book, the date of its writing must be before his death in 450 AH (1058 CE).

No manuscript of the essay is available. However, there is an essay under "Mā lā-yasaʿ al-mukallaf jahluh" (What the duty-bound person cannot ignore) in the list of manuscripts of the library of Kāshif al-Ghiṭāʾ Public Library (manuscript number: 1080) in forty-five pages, which might be the same as this work (Āqā Buzurg Ṭihrānī 1403AH, 19:26-7).[1] This manuscript begins with the problem of incipience (*ḥudūth*) of physical objects, and is concerned with principles of religious beliefs (ibid).

The essay is mentioned in the following classical bibliographies: Ṭūsī's *al-Fihrist* (n.d., 160), Najāshī's *Rijāl* (1365 SH, 403), Ibn Shahrāshūb's *Maʿālim al-ʿulamāʾ* (1380AH, 115), and Āqā Buzurg Ṭihrānī's *al-Dharīʿa* (1403 AH, 19:26-7).

10. Al-Masāʾil al-kalāmiyya (A)

"The theological problems" is a work attributed to Ṭūsī. It is not mentioned by Ṭūsī in his own *al-Fihrist*, nor by Najāshī. Āqā Buzurg Ṭihrānī mentions the book in his *al-Dharīʿa* with the above title (1403AH, 20:364), and also under "Masāʾil kalāmiyya" (ibid., 5:9). It is also mentioned as "Masāʾil al-tawḥīd" (Problems of monotheism) (Dirāyatī 1390 SH, 29:255).

This is a short theological essay encompassing about thirty problems in various issues such as monotheism, justice, prophethood, and imamate. There are differences in different manuscripts in the number of problems, as they amount to more than thirty in certain manuscripts,

1 For more information on this, see https://scripts.nlai.ir/.

but this comes down to different ways of counting the issues (Dirāyatī, 1390 SH, 9:713). The essay is not structured into parts and chapters. It has been published in *al-Rasā'il al-'ashr* in eight pages.

The book is mentioned in the following classical bibliography: Āqā Buzurg Ṭihrānī's *al-Dharī'a* (1403 AH, 20:364; 5:9; and 14:64).

A manuscript of the book is available in the Library of Ayatollah Mar'ashī Najafī (manuscript number: 14310/4). It is written in four pages, but the scribe is not known. It was transcribed in the tenth century AH (sixteenth century CE).

The book has been critically edited and published by Jāmi'i Mudarrisīn in Qom in 1414 AH.

There are commentaries and glossaries written for this book:

1. "Khulāṣat al-wasā'il fī sharḥ al-masā'il": This is an Arabic exposition of the book, of which only one manuscript has been found, but the identity of its author is not known, as the first page of the manuscript is missing. Of this manuscript, only twenty-eight pages have survived, and the second page only features the title of the book.
2. "Sharḥ masā'il kalāmiyya" by Sayyid 'Azīz Allāh Ḥusaynī, a teacher in the mausoleum of Shaykh Ṣafī in Ardabil, Iran. This is an Arabic exposition, of which one manuscript is available in the Library of Astan Quds Razavi in Mashhad, Iran.
3. "Sharḥ masā'il kalāmiyya": This is the style of commentaries in the form of, "he said" followed by first sentences of each problem and a commentary. The author has not been identified. A twelve-page manuscript of the work is available in a collection in the Library of Raḍawiyya Seminary School in Qom, Iran.

11. Muqaddima fi l-madkhal ilā ʿilm al-kalām (D)

"An introduction to the entry into the science of theology" is a theological essay. Ṭūsī mentions it in his own *al-Fihrist* (n.d., 161), where he says that such a work is unprecedented. Ṭūsī also wrote an exposition for the essay, to which Najāshī (1365 SH, 403) refers as "Riyāḍat al-ʿuqūl" (Exercise of reasons). Āqā Buzurg Ṭihrānī introduces several manuscripts of the book in his *al-Dharīʿa* (1403 AH, 22:92). Despite the consensus over the attribution of the title to Ṭūsī, some researchers believe that no manuscript is available of this work (Adībīmihr 1384 SH, 146). Others believe that some of the manuscripts cited in *al-Dharīʿa* are indeed manuscripts of Ṭūsī's *Risāla fi l-iʿtiqādāt*, and the manuscript in the Library of Mishkat belongs to *Muqaddima fi l-madkhal* (Rawḍātī 1354 SH, 722).

Ṭūsī dictated the essay at the demand of some of his students (as he points out in the introduction of the essay). The essay has been published in *al-Rasāʾil al-ʿashr* in twenty-eight pages (Ṭūsī 1414 AH, 63ff). It is structured into six chapters, the first of which deals with the common terminology used by theologians. It is followed by problems concerning kinds of existence, kinds of accidents (*aʿrāḍ*), the nature and features of attributes, the nature of reason and certain problems pertaining to it, and the nature and kinds of acts.

The writing of the essay was finished in 444 AH (1052 CE), as the scribe of the manuscript, Niẓām al-Dīn Maḥmūd ibn ʿAlī al-Khwārazmī, dates it Rajab 26, 444 AH/ November 21, 1052 CE (Wāʿiẓzāda 1363 SH, 32). Moreover, Ṭūsī's written permission on the back of this manuscript dates Muharram 26, 445 (May 18, 1053). This information also shows that Ṭūsī was in Dār al-Salām in the suburbs of Baghdad around this date (Wāʿiẓzāda 1363 SH, 32).

The essay is mentioned in the following classical bibliographies: Najāshī's *Rijāl* (1365 SH, 403), Ibn Shahrāshūb's *Maʿālim al-ʿulamāʾ* (1380 AH, 115), Āqā Buzurg Ṭihrānī's *al-Dharīʿa* (1403 AH, 22:91-2).

Two manuscripts of the book are available in Malik library in Tehran, Iran. One dates back to the tenth century AH (sixteenth century CE) under manuscript number 5712/8, and the other dates back to the eighth century AH (eighteenth century CE) under manuscript number 458.

The essay has been critically edited and published in *al-Rasāʾil al-ʿashr (The ten essays)* by Jāmiʿi Mudarrisīn in Qom in 1414 AH.

3.1.4. Missing Works

12. Al-Kāfī (C)

"The sufficient" is a book of theology, of which limited information is available in bibliographies. It does not appear in books of rijāl and even a bibliography as comprehensive as *al-Dharīʿa*. The only information about the book is in Ibn Shahrāshūb's *Maʿālim al-ʿulamāʾ* where he says that the book was unfinished (1380 AH, 103). The latter comment by Ibn Shahrāshūb is evidence that he had access to a manuscript, or perhaps several manuscripts, of the work not available to his contemporaries. No book manuscript is available to us either (Adībīmihr 1384 SH, 139).

Thus, of classical bibliographies, the essay is only cited in Ibn Shahrāshūb's *Maʿālim al-ʿulamāʾ* (1380 AH, 115).

13. Uṣūl al-ʿaqāʾid (C)

"Principles of beliefs" is an unfinished essay concerning monotheism and justice, which Ṭūsī cites in his *al-Fihrist*: "he [Ṭūsī] has a voluminous book concerning the principles, of which the material about monotheism and some about justice have come out" (Ṭūsī n.d.,

161). It is also referred to as “Risāla fi l-iʿtiqādāt” (Essay on beliefs) (Adībīmihr 1384 SH, 132). Some people believe that this is the same as “Sharḥ al-shurūḥ fi l-uṣūl” (Exposition of expositions on principles) (Wāʿiẓzāda 1363 SH, 44), which does not appear in Ṭūsī’s *al-Fihrist*. Āqā Buzurg Ṭihrānī explicitly separates the two works in his *al-Dharīʿa* (1403AH, 2:198). No information is available on manuscripts or published versions of the book.

Of classical bibliographies, the work is cited in Ṭūsī’s own *al-Fihrist* (n.d., 161), and Āqā Buzurg Ṭihrānī’s *al-Dharīʿa* (1403 AH, 2:198).

14. Al-Istīfāʾ fi l-imāma (C)

“The fulfillment on imamate” is a theological essay concerning imamate. This work is cited by Ṭūsī himself in another work of his *al-Mufaṣṣiḥ* (in *al-Rasāʾil al-ʿashr*, 1414 AH, 129), which implies that it was written during the lifetime of Sayyid Murtaḍā before the writing of *al-Mufaṣṣiḥ*. Some people believe that this is the same as *Talkhīṣ al-shāfī* (Kohlberg, 316). This is probably grounded in a mistake by the scribe of *Talkhīṣ al-shāfī* who added the term “fulfillment” on the cover of the manuscript, presumably based on a statement in the introduction of the work where Ṭūsī says, “its fulfillment (*Istīfāʾ*) is inevitable” (Āqā Buzurg Ṭihrānī, 2:36). In addition, the essay is cited by Ṭūsī in his *al-Mufaṣṣiḥ* as “Al-Istīfāʾ fi l-imāma” (p. 129), which can be another evidence that these are distinct works. Nevertheless, one might cast doubts over their distinction in that the work does not appear in Najāshī’s *Rijāl* and Ṭūsī’s own *al-Fihrist*, although this work was purportedly written early in Ṭūsī’s career (Riḍādād and Ṭabāṭabāʾī 1387 SH, 58-59).

Of classical bibliographies, the work is mentioned in Āqā Buzurg Ṭihrānī’s *al-Dharīʿa* (1403 AH, 2:37).

15. Al-Masāʾil al-Rāziyya fi l-waʿīd (C)

"Questions from Rey about the divine threat" is mentioned by Ṭūsī in his own *al-Fihrist* (n.d., 161). It is also referred to as "al-Mas'alat al-Rāziyya fi l-waʿīd" (The question from Rey about the divine threat) (Ibn Shahrāshūb 1380 AH, 115) and "Jawābāt al-masā'il al-Rāziyya" (Replies to questions from Rey) (Āqā Buzurg Ṭihrānī 1403 AH, 5:221).

The work is concerned with the problem of the divine threat (*waʿīd*), including 15 questions asked by a scholar from Rey in Iran from Sayyid Murtaḍā (Ṭūsī's teacher) to which Sayyid replied, but Ṭūsī also replied to those questions (Āqā Buzurg 1376 SH, 58). The writing of the essay dates to a time before 436 AH (1044 CE); that is, during the lifetime of Sayyid Murtaḍā (Riḍādād and Ṭabāṭabā'ī 1387 SH, 61).

No manuscript of the book has so far been found. It should be noted that the questions published in a collection of Sayyid Murtaḍā's essays under "al-Masāʾil al-Rāziyya" (Questions from Rey) are not concerned with the divine threat. Thus, it cannot be attributed to Ṭūsī (Riḍādād and Ṭabāṭabā'ī 1387 AH, 61).

The work is mentioned in the following classical bibliographies: Ṭūsī's *al-Fihrist* (n.d., 161), Ibn Shahrāshūb's *Maʿālim al-ʿulamāʾ* (1380AH, 115), and Āqā Buzurg Ṭihrānī's *al-Dharīʿa* (1403 AH, 5:20).

16. Mā yuʿallal wa-mā lā-yuʿallal (C)

"What is explained and what is not explained" is a work mentioned by Ṭūsī in his own *al-Fihrist* (n.d., 161). It has been claimed that it is concerned with theology (Āqā Buzurg Ṭihrānī 1376 SH, 54; Amīn 1403 AH, 9:166), but some people vacillate between jurisprudence and theology (Wāʿiẓzāda 1363 SH, 42). Since Najāshī has also mentions the work, it must have been written before his death in 450 AH (1058 CE). No information is available of manuscripts of the work.

The work is mentioned in the following classical bibliographies: Najāshī's *Rijāl* (1365 SH, 403) and Āqā Buzurg Ṭihrānī's *al-Dharī'a* (1403 AH, 19:36).

17. Riyāḍat al-'uqūl (C)

"Exercise of reasons" is a work by Ṭūsī also known as "Sharḥ al-muqaddima fi l-madkhal ilā 'ilm al-kalām" (Exposition of the introduction to the entry into the science of theology). It is mentioned by Ṭūsī in his *al-Fihrist* as follows: "he [Ṭūsī] has an introduction to the entry into the science of theology the like of which was not done by anyone, and he has an exposition for this introduction" (n.d., 161). Najāshī and Ibn Shahrāshūb refer to the essay as "Riyāḍat al-'uqūl" (Najāshī 1365 SH, 403; Ibn Shahrāshūb 1380 AH, 115). This is a theological essay written as an exposition of another work by Ṭūsī himself under "Muqaddima fi l-madkhal ilā 'ilm al-kalām" (An introduction to the entry into the science of theology).

Some people have speculated that the writing of the book dates to the years between 445 AH (1053 CE) and 450 AH (1058 CE) (Riḍādād and Ṭabāṭabā'ī 1387 SH, 65). No manuscript of the essay has so far been found.

The essay is mentioned in the following classical bibliographies: Ṭūsī's *al-Fihrist* (n.d., 161), Najāshī's *Rijāl* (1365 SH, 403), Ibn Shahrāshūb's *Ma'ālim al-'ulamā'* (1380 AH, 115), and Āqā Buzurg Ṭihrānī's *al-Dharī'a* (1403 AH, 11:340).

18. Al-Naqḍ 'alā Ibn Shādhān fī mas'alat al-ghār (C)

"The refutation of Ibn Shādhān over the problem of the cave" is a theological work by Ṭūsī, mentioned by him in his own *al-Fihrist* (n.d., 161). It is also noted by Ibn Shahrāshūb (1380 AH, 115). This seems to be an essay concerning the problem of Abū Bakr's companionship with Prophet Muḥammad in a cave during his escape from Mecca to Medina. According to Āqā Buzurg Ṭihrānī's quote from Sayyid Mahdī Baḥr al-ʿUlūm, the essay also deals with the problem of *khabar al-wāḥid* (whether reports by single narrators are reliable), which is evidence that Baḥr al-ʿUlūm had access to a manuscript of the work (Āqā Buzurg Ṭihrānī 1403AH, 24:287). No information is available of manuscripts of the work. Since the work has not been mentioned by Najāshī (d. 450 AH/1058 CE) but is mentioned towards the end of Ṭūsī's *al-Fihrist*, it has been speculated that it was written after Najāshī's death in 450 AH (1058 CE); that is, during the last decade of Ṭūsī's life (Riḍādād and Ṭabāṭabāʾī 1387 SH, 67).

The work is mentioned in the following classical bibliographies: Ṭūsī's *al-Fihrist* (n.d., 161) and Āqā Buzurg Ṭihrānī's *al-Dharīʿa* (1403 AH, 24:287).

❖

3.2. Jurisprudence (Fiqh)

3.2.1. Miscellaneous

19. Al-Jumal wa-l-ʿuqūd fi l-ʿibādāt (A)

"The sentences and nodes about worships" is a work by Ṭūsī. It is mentioned by Ṭūsī himself in his *al-Fihrist* (n.d., 161), Najāshī (1365 SH, 403), and Ibn Shahrāshūb (1380 AH, 115). This is brief well-organized about worships—from issues of cleanliness (*ṭahāra*) to enjoining the right and forbidding the wrong (*al-amr bi-l-maʿrūf wa-l-nahy ʿan al-munkar*). It is written at the request of Qāḍī Ibn Barrāj (d.

481 AH/1088 CE), a student of Ṭūsī and his representative in the Levant (Āqā Buzurg Ṭihrānī 1403 AH, 5:145). Ṭūsī finished writing this jurisprudential essay before he finished writing his *al-Mabsūṭ* (which is cited in this essay: Ṭūsī 1414 AH). It has been published in *al-Rasā'il al-'ashr.*

The essay is mentioned in the following classical bibliographies: Ṭūsī's *al-Fihrist* (n.d., 161), Najāshī's *Rijāl* (1365 SH, 403), Ibn Shahrāshūb's *Ma'ālim al-'ulamā'* (1380 AH, 115), and Āqā Buzurg Ṭihrānī's *al-Dharī'a* (1403 AH, 5:145).

A photographed manuscript of the essay is available in Markaz Iḥyā' in Qom, Iran. The original manuscript is held in the Library of Kāshif al-Ghiṭā' in Najaf, Iraq. It was written in 132 pages, but the scribe is not known. The manuscript was written on Thursday Rabi' I 15, 723 AH (March 24, 1323 CE).

The essay was critically edited by Mahdī Najaf and published by Dār al-Mufīd in Qom in 1413AH.

A commentary was written on the essay by Muḥaqqiq Ḥillī Ja'far ibn Ḥasan (602 AH/1205 CE - 676 AH/1277 CE) under *al-Jumal wa-l-'uqūd (The sentences and nodes).*

20. Al-Mabsūṭ fī fiqh al-Imāmiyya (A)

"The elaborate in Imami jurisprudence" is a well-known jurisprudential book by Ṭūsī. It was mentioned by Ṭūsī in his own *al-Fihrist* (n.d., 160) and Ibn Shahrāshūb (1380 AH, 115). This is a lengthy book in argumentative jurisprudence, including seventy sections from cleanliness (*ṭahāra*) to blood money (*diyāt*). Ṭūsī himself says that the book involves 80 sections, but this seems to be a slip of pen either by him or by the scribes (Adībīmihr 1384 SH, 139). Ṭūsī's motivation for writing the book was that other Islamic sects accused Imamis of not having an elaborate jurisprudential system, saying that Shiite jurists only reject the theories of other jurisprudential denominations on account of their negation of principles such as *qiyās* (analogy) and ijtihad. Thus, Ṭūsī decided to present an elaborate jurisprudential system by writing *al-Mabsūṭ* (as he makes it explicit in the preface of the book: Ṭūsī 1387 AH, 2). He characterizes this book as a unique work of his own (ibid, 3).

This seems to be the last elaborate jurisprudential work written by Ṭūsī, which was arguably written simultaneously with his *Miṣbāḥ al-mutahajjid* (Riḍādād and Ṭabāṭabā'ī 1387 SH, 63). This book has been published in eight volumes.

The book is mentioned in the following classical bibliographies: Ṭūsī's *al-Fihrist* (n.d., 160), Ibn Shahrāshūb's *Ma'ālim al-'ulamā'* (1380 AH, 115), and Āqā Buzurg Ṭihrānī's *al-Dharī'a* (1403 AH, 19:54).

A manuscript of the book is available in the Library of Ayatollah Gulpāyigānī in Qom, Iran (manuscript number: 1/46-46). It was written in 162 pages, probably in the ninth century AH (fifteenth century CE), but its scribe is unknown. The manuscript is not complete, as it covers the section on cleanliness all the way through the section on peace. Another manuscript of the book is available in Markaz Iḥyā' in Qom, Iran (manuscript number: 3852). It was written in 146 pages in the eleventh century AH (seventeenth century CE), but the scribe is unknown. This manuscript is also incomplete, covering from the section on *musāqāt* (irrigation contract) through the section on marriage. A complete manuscript of the book is available in the Library of Shaykh Muḥammad Qawānīnī Burūjirdī with the handwriting of Ḥusayn ibn Muḥammad Ja'far Khwānsārī in 1230 AH (1815 CE).

The book has been critically edited and published in eight volumes by Murtaḍawī Publications in Tehran in 1387 AH.

21. Al-Masā'il al-Ḥā'iriyya (A)

"Questions from Ḥā'ir" is a work by Ṭūsī, which he mentions in his own *al-Fihrist* (n.d., 161). In different sources, it has been referred to as "al-Ḥā'iriyyāt" as well (Adībīmihr 1384 SH, 144). The essay was written in response to questions concerning various theological, exegetical, and jurisprudential questions asked by people of al-Ḥā'ir al-Ḥusaynī (i.e., Karbala) (Dirāyatī 1390 SH, 29:257). In the part on jurisprudential questions and replies, issues about marriage, transaction, khums, fasting, prayer, *qiṣāṣ* (retaliatory punishment for murder), divorce, zakat, and the like are raised in an unorganized way. In his *al-Fihrist*, Ṭūsī points out that the essay contains 300 questions (n.d., 161), but in the available manuscripts there are around 150 questions, and thus, they should all be seen as incomplete (Dirāyatī 1390 SH, 29:257). This is evidenced by the fact that some of the questions quoted by Ibn Idrīs (d. 598 AH/1201 CE) are not found in available manuscripts (Mu'assisa Nūr 1391 SH, under *al-Rasā'il al-ʿashr*).

Although Ibn Shahrāshūb does not mention the title, he cites an essay under "al-Masā'il al-jabriyya" including around 300 questions (1380 AH, 115), which might be the same as this work (Adībīmihr 1384 SH, 144).

The work is mentioned in the following classical bibliographies: Ṭūsī's *al-Fihrist* (n.d., 161) and Āqā Buzurg Ṭihrānī's *al-Dharīʿa* (1403 AH, 5:218).

A manuscript of the essay is available in the Library of Ayatollah Marʿashī Najafī (manuscript number: 12747/5). This was written in 14 pages in the twelfth century AH (eighteenth century CE), but its scribe is unknown.

The essay has been critically edited and published in *al-Rasā'il al-ʿashr (The ten essays)* by Jāmiʿi Mudarrisīn in Qom in 1414 AH.

22. Al-nihāya fī mujarrad al-fiqh wa-l-fatāwā (A)

"The ultimate in pure jurisprudence and fatwas" is a book by Ṭūsī, which is mentioned by him himself in his own *al-Fihrist* (n.d., 160), by Najāshī (1365 SH, 403), and by Ibn Shahrāshūb (1380 AH, 115). This is a complete survey of fatwa-based jurisprudence from the issues of cleanliness (*ṭahāra*) to those of blood money (*diyāt*), and just like *al-Muqniʿ* by Shaykh Ṣadūq (d. 380 AH/ 991CE) and *al-Muqniʿa* by Shaykh Mufīd (d. 413 AH/1022 CE), it consists of excerpts of hadith texts, which is called "textual jurisprudence" (*al-fiqh al-manṣūṣ*) or "received principles" (*uṣūl mutalaqqāt*). Since Ṭūsī's lifetime until the lifetime of Muḥaqqiq Ḥillī, the book was the center of discussions, research, and teachings. It counted as the only document for permissions of transmissions, but after Muḥaqqiq Ḥillī's time (d. 676 AH/1277 CE), *Sharāʾiʿ al-islām* assumed the status (Āqā Buzurg Ṭihrānī 1376 SH, 63).

According to Āqā Buzurg Ṭihrānī's enumeration of a manuscript, the essay includes twenty-two parts, 214 sections, and 36000 problems. Some researchers believe that this is the second writing by Āqā Buzurg (Riḍādād and Ṭabāṭabāʾī 1387 SH, 57). Appealing to evidence such as the essay's reference to *Tahdhīb al-aḥkām* and the fact that it was written during the lifetime of Sayyid Murtaḍā (d. 436 AH/1044 CE), some researchers believe that it was written between 415 AH/1024 CE and 435 AC/1043 CE (Mu'assasa Nūr 1391 SH, under *al-Nihāya fī mujarrad al-fiqh wa-l-fatāwā*). This book has been published in one volume of 782 pages.

The book is mentioned in the following classical bibliographies: Ṭūsī's *al-Fihrist* (n.d., 160), Najāshī's *Rijāl* (1365 SH, 403), Ibn Shahrāshūb's *Maʿālim al-ʿulamāʾ* (1380 AH, 115), and Āqā Buzurg Ṭihrānī's *al-Dharīʿa* (1403 AH, 24:403).

A manuscript of the book is available in the Library of Astan Quds Razavi in Mashhad, Iran (manuscript number: 17581). Yaḥyā ibn

Aḥmad Raḥla transcribed the manuscript in Muharram 538 AH (July 1143 CE).

The book was critically edited and published by Dār al-Kitāb al-ʿArabī in Beirut in 1400 AH, and by Muḥammad Taqī Dānishpazhūh, which is published by University of Tehran Press in 1360 SH.

The book has been translated into Persian by Muḥammad Bāqir Sabzawārī and published by University of Tehran Press in 1362 SH.

It has been translated into English as *Al-Nihaya fi Mujarrad al-Fiqh wa al-Fatwa: A Concise Description of Islamic Law and Legal Opinions*, trans. A. Ezzati, London: ICAS Press, 2008.

Many commentaries and glossaries have been written for the book:

1. *Nukat al-nihāya* (Points of *al-Nihāya*) or *Ḥall mushkilāt al-nihāya* (The solution to the problems of *al-Nihāya)* and *Sharḥ mushkilāt al-nihāya* (Exposition of the problems of *al-Nihāya*) by Muḥaqqiq Ḥillī (d. 676 AH/1277 CE).
2. *Al-Murshid ilā sabīl al-taʿabbud* (The guide to the path of servitude) by Ṭūsī's son Abū ʿAlī Ḥasan ibn Muḥammad Ṭūsī (alive in 515 AH/1121 CE).
3. *Sharḥ al-nihāya* (Exposition of *al-Nihāya*), by Niẓām al-Dīn Sulaymān ibn Ḥasan Ṣahrashtī (d. later in the fifth century AH (eleventh century CE).
4. *Sharḥ mushkilāt al-nihāya* (Exposition of the problems of *al-Nihāya*), by Quṭb al-Dīn Rāwandī (d. 573 AH/1177 CE).
5. *Sharḥ mā yajūz wa-mā lā-yajūz fī l-nihāya* (Exposition of what is allowed and what is not allowed in *al-Nihāya*), by Quṭb al-Dīn Rāwandī (d. 573 AH/1177 CE).
6. *Nihāyat al-nihāya* (The ultimate of the ultimate), by Quṭb al-Dīn Rāwandī (d. 573 AH/1177 CE).

7. *Al-Mughnī fī sharḥ al-nihāyat al-Ṭūsiyya* (The enricher in exposition of Ṭūsī's *al-Nihāya*), by Quṭb al-Dīn Rāwandī (d. 573 AH/1177 CE).

23. Masā'il al-khilāf ma' al-kull fi l-fiqh (A)

"Problems of disagreement with all in jurisprudence" is a jurisprudential work by Ṭūsī. It is mentioned with the above title by Ṭūsī in his *Al-fihrist* (n.d., 161) and Ibn Shahrāshūb (1380 AH, 115). It is mentioned in some sources as "al-Khilāf fi l-aḥkām" (The disagreement in rulings) (see Āqā Buzurg Ṭihrānī's *al-Dharī'a*, 1403 AH, 7:235). This is a book about comparative jurisprudence written at the request of some people (see the preface of the book: Ṭūsī 1407 AH, 45). It encompasses the whole jurisprudence from cleanliness (*ṭahāra*) to blood money (*diyāt*). It addresses problems over which Imami jurisprudence disagrees with other denominations. It first states the views of other denominations concerning a specific problem and then articulates arguments for the Imami position in that connection. This might be described as the first comprehensive work of comparative jurisprudence.

Ṭūsī says that he wrote the book after *al-Tahdhīb* and *al-Istibṣār* (1407 AH, 1:46; also see Āqā Buzurg Ṭihrānī 1403 AH, 7:235). Since *al-Mabsūṭ* is once cited in *al-Khilāf*, some people believe that the former was written *al-Khilāf* was being finished (Riḍādād and Ṭabāṭabā'ī 1387 SH, 63). The book has been published in six volumes.

Al-Khilāf is mentioned in the following classical bibliographies: Ṭūsī's *al-Fihrist* (n.d., 161), Ibn Shahrāshūb's *Ma'ālim al-'ulamā'* (1380AH, 115), Āqā Buzurg Ṭihrānī's *al-Dharī'a* (1403 AH, 7:235).

A complete manuscript of the book is available in the Library of the Department of Theology at Tehran University in Tehran, Iran (manuscript number: 41). It was written in 381 pages by Muḥammad

ʿAlī ibn Muḥammad Qāsim on Tuesday Dhu al-Hijja 13, 1244 AH (June 16, 1829 CE). Most other manuscripts of the book are incomplete.

The book has been critically edited and published in six volumes by Jāmiʿi Mudarrisīn in Qom in 1407 AH.

Commentaries and summaries have been written for the book, including:

1. *Masāʾil al-khilāf* (Problems of disagreement) or *al-Muntakhab min masāʾil al-khilāf* (The selection of problems of disagreement) or *al-Muʾtalaf min al-mukhtalaf* (The combination from the disagreement) by Faḍl ibn Ḥasan Ṭabarsī (468 AH/1073 CE - 548 AH/1154 CE).
2. *Masāʾil al-khilāf* (Problems of disagreement) or *Talkhīṣ al-khilāf wa-khulāṣat al-ikhtilāf* (Summary of the disagreement and synopsis of the dispute), Mufliḥ ibn Ḥasan Ṣaymarī (d. 900 AC/1494 CE).
3. *Ḥāshiyat al-khilāf fi l-aḥkām* (Commentary on the disagreement in rulings) by Aḥmad ibn ʿInāyat Allāh (1308 AH/1890 CE - 1393 AH/1973 CE).

3.2.2. Inheritance

24. Al-Ījāz fi l-farāʾiḍ (A)

"The brief on heritages" is a work mentioned by Ṭūsī himself in his *al-Fihrist* (n.d., 161), Najāshī (1365 SH, 403), and Ibn Shahrāshūb (1380AH, 115). It is known as "al-Munāsakhāt fi l-irth" (Hereditary hierarchies on inheritance" (Dirāyatī 1380 SH, 5:436) and "Mukhtaṣar fi l-farāʾiḍ wa-l-mawārīth" (The brief in heritages and inheritance) as well (Adībīmihr 1384 SH, 133).

This is a brief essay concerning the rulings of inheritance, at many points in which Ṭūsī refers the reader to his *al-Nihāya* for further details (Muʾassasa Nūr 1391 SH). For this reason, some researchers believe that the essay was written before *al-Mabsūṭ*; otherwise, Ṭūsī would refer the reader to *al-Mabsūṭ* which involves much more details (Riḍādād and Ṭabāṭabāʾī 1387 SH, 62). The essay has been published in *Al-Rasāʾil al-ʿashr*.

"Al-Ījāz fi l-farāʾiḍ" is mentioned in the following classical bibliographies: Ṭūsī's *al-Fihrist* (n.d., 161), Najāshī's *Rijāl* (1365SH, 403), Ibn Shahrāshūb's *Maʿālim al-ʿulamāʾ* (1380 AH, 115), and Āqā Buzurg Ṭihrānī's *al-Dharīʿa* (1403 AH, 2:486).

A manuscript of the work is available in the National Library of Iran in Tehran (manuscript number: 1943/9). It is written by Muḥammad Mufīd ibn Muḥammad Taqī Ḥusaynī in 1085 AH (1674 CE).

The essay is critically edited and published by Jāmiʿi Mudarrisīn in Qom in 1414 AH.

Quṭb al-Dīn Rāwandī (d. 572 AH/1177 CE) wrote a commentary on the essay under "al-Iʿjāz fī sharḥ al-ījāz fi l-farāʾiḍ" (The accomplishment in the exposition of the brief in heritages).

3.2.3. Others

25. Masʾala fī taḥrīm al-fuqāʿ (A)

"A problem about the forbiddance of beer" is an essay by Ṭūsī, which he mentions in his *al-Fihrist* (n.d., 161). In this essay, he briefly deals with Sunni and Shiite views of the jurisprudential ruling of drinking beer, as well as their arguments. Moreover, he touches on certain issues in the "principles of jurisprudence" such as conflicts between hadiths, reliability of consensus (*ijmāʿ*), and the like. As in its opening lines of the work, the problem of beer was first raised in the presence of a contemporary Buyid king, and then Ṭūsī decided to elaborate on it. The king seems to be a Buyid king contemporary with Ṭūsī, who ruled between 436 AH/1044 CE (Sayyid Murtaḍā's death) and 447 AH/1055 CE (when Tughril Beg conquered Baghdad)—a period when Ṭūsī was in Baghdad under the auspicious of the Buyid dynasty. On this account, the essay was probably written between these years (Mu'assasa Nūr 1391 SH, under *al-Rasā'il al-ʿashr*).

The essay is mentioned in the following classical bibliographies: Ṭūsī's *al-Fihrist* (n.d., 161) and Āqā Buzurg Ṭihrānī's *al-Dharīʿa* (1403 AH, 20: 385).

A manuscript of the essay is available in the Library of Astan Quds Razavi in Mashhad, Iran (manuscript number: ḍ33039). It was transcribed in five pages in the late thirteenth century AH (nineteenth century CE), but the scribe is not known. Another manuscript is available in the Library of Ayatollah Marʿashī Najafī (manuscript number: 1104/6).

The essay has been critically edited and published in *al-Rasā'il al-ʿashr* published by Jāmiʿi Mudarrisīn in Qom in 1414 AH.

26. Mukhtaṣar fī ʿamal yawm wa-layla (A)

"The brief in acts of day and night" is a work by Ṭūsī, which he mentions in his *al-Fihrist* (n.d., 161). In some sources, it is cited as "ʿAmal al-yawm wa-l-layla" (Act of the day and the night) as well (Dirāyatī 1390SH, 22:2007; Āqā Buzurg Ṭihrānī 1403AH, 15:349). This is a jurisprudential essay concerning prayer (*ṣalāt*) written at the request of Sayyid Murtaḍā (d. 436 AH/1044 CE), as Ṭūsī says in his preface to the essay (Ṭūsī 1414 AH, 141). The essay contains eight chapters in which he briefly addresses issues pertaining to prayer, such as acts and conditions of prayer, cleanliness, time, *qibla*, place, clothes, and obligatory and supererogatory prayers. It has been published in *al-Rasā'il al-'ashr* in twelve pages. Some researchers argue that it was written before writing *Miṣbāḥ*; that is, before 448 AH/1056 CE (Riḍādād and Ṭabāṭabā'ī 1387 SH, 65), and others believe that it was written between 430 AH/1038 CE and 436 AH/1044 CE; that is, late in Sayyid Murtaḍā's life (Mu'assasa Nūr 1391 SH, under *al-Rasā'il al-'ashr*).

The essay is mentioned in the following classical bibliographies: Ṭūsī's *al-Fihrist* (n.d., 161) and Āqā Buzurg Ṭihrānī's *al-Dharī'a* (1403 AH, 15:349).

A manuscript of the essay is available in the Library of Majlis in Tehran, Iran (manuscript number: 711/5). It was written in seven pages by 'Alī Riḍā ibn Muḥammad Ghiyāth Shūlistānī in 1068 AH/1657 CE.

The essay is critically edited and published in *al-Rasā'il al-'ashr* by Jāmi'i Mudarrisīn in Qom in 1414 AH.

3.2.4. Missing Works

27. Al-Masā'il al-Junbalā'iyya (C)

"Questions from Junbalā'" is a set of questions and replies by Ṭūsī, which he mentions in his *al-Fihrist* (n.d., 160). It is also mentioned by Ibn Shahrāshūb (1380 AH, 115). In some manuscripts, its title is "al-Jaylāniyya" but Āqā Buzurg Ṭihrānī believes that the former is nearer to the mark (1403 AH, 20:343). In *al-Dharī'a* (Ṭihrānī 1403 AH, 5:218), it is also referred to as "Jawābāt al-masā'il al-Junbalā'iyya" (Replies to questions from Junbalā'). This is a jurisprudential essay including twenty-four questions, but no manuscript of it has so far been found.

The essay is mentioned in the following classical bibliographies: Ṭūsī's *al-Fihrist* (n.d., 160), Ibn Shahrāshūb's *Ma'ālim al-'ulamā'* (1380 AH, 115), and Āqā Buzurg Ṭihrānī's *al-Dharī'a* (1403 AH, 5:218).

28. Al-Masā'il al-Ḥalabiyya (C)

"Questions from Aleppo" is a set of questions and replies by Ṭūsī, which Ṭūsī mentions in his *al-Fihrist* (n.d., 161). It is also mentioned by Ibn Shahrāshūb (1380 AH, 115). In *al-Dharī'a*, Āqā Buzurg Ṭihrānī also refers to it as "Jawābāt al-masā'il al-Ḥalabiyya" (Replies to questions from Aleppo) (Ṭihrānī 1403 AH, 5:219). This is a jurisprudential essay in reply to questions from Aleppo as the title suggests (Āqā Buzurg Ṭihrānī 1376 SH, 58). No manuscript of the essay has so far been found).

It is mentioned in the following classical bibliographies: Ṭūsī's *al-Fihrist* (n.d., 160), Ibn Shahrāshūb's *Ma'ālim al-'ulamā'* (1380 AH, 115), and Ṭihrānī's *al-Dharī'a* (1403 AH, 5:219).

29. Masā'il Ibn al-Barrāj (C)

"Questions of Ibn al-Barrāj" is a set of questions and replies by Ṭūsī. It is mentioned by Ibn Shahrāshūb (1380 AH, 115). Āqā Buzurg Ṭihrānī claims that the essay is also mentioned in Ṭūsī's *al-Fihrist* as well (1403 AH, 20:331), but the essay is not mentioned in the version of the work edited by Baḥr al-'Ulūm (n.d., Najaf: Maktabat al-Murtaḍawiyya). Since the questions are asked by Qāḍī Ibn Barrāj (d. 481 AH/1088 CE), who was a jurist, the essay is probably concerned with jurisprudence. No manuscript of the essay is available.

The essay is mentioned in the following classical bibliographies: Ibn Shahrāshūb's *Ma'ālim al-'ulamā'* (1380 AH, 115) and Āqā Buzurg Ṭihrānī's *al-Dharī'a* (1403 AH, 20:331).

30. Mas'ala fī mawāqīt al-ṣalāt (C)

"A problem about the times of prayer" is an essay attributed to Ṭūsī by Ibn Shahrāshūb (1380 AH, 115), but it is not listed in any other biography or bibliography of Ṭūsī. As the title suggests, it is a jurisprudential essay concerning the times of prayer. No manuscript of the essay is available.

Of classical bibliographies, the essay is only mentioned in Ibn Shahrāshūb's *Ma'ālim al-'ulamā'* (1380 AH, 115).

31. Mas'ala fī wujūb al-jizya 'ala-l-Yahūd wa-l-muntamīn ila-l-jabābira (al-khayābira) (C)

"A problem about the obligation of *jizya* [taxation] for Jews and those who belong to tyrants" is an essay by Ṭūsī. It is mentioned in some manuscripts of Ṭūsī's *al-Fihrist* (1420 AH, 451). It is also mentioned by Ibn Shahrāshūb (1380 AH, 115). In some sources, it is known as "Mas'ala fī wujūb al-jizya 'ala-l-Yahūd wa-l-mushimīn ila-l-janā'iz" (A problem about the obligation of *jizya* for Jews and contributors to funerals) as well (Adībīmihr 1384 SH, 142). As its title suggests, it is a jurisprudential essay concerning *jizya* (taxation on non-Muslims). No manuscript of the essay is available.

The essay is mentioned by Ṭūsī in his *al-Fihrist* (1420AH, 451) and Āqā Buzurg Ṭihrānī in his *al-Dharī'a* (1403 AH, 20:397).

32. Manāsik al-ḥajj fī mujarrad al-ʿamal wa-l-adʿiya (C)

"Rituals of hajj only in the act and supplications" is a work by Ṭūsī, which he mentions in his *al-Fihrist* (n.d., 161). It is also mentioned by Ibn Shahrāshūb (1380 AH, 115). As its title suggests, it is a jurisprudential essay concerning hajj. No manuscript of the essay is available.

Appealing to the fact that the work is not mentioned by Najāshī (d. 450 AH/1058 CE) and that it is mentioned toward the end of Ṭūsī's *al-Fihrist*, it has been speculated that it might be have been written after Najāshī's death; that is, in the last decade of Ṭūsī's life (Riḍādād and Ṭabāṭabā'ī 1387 SH, 67).

The work is mentioned in the following classical bibliographies: Ṭūsī's *al-Fihrist* (n.d., 161), Ibn Shahrāshūb's *Maʿālim al-ʿulamā'* (1380 AH, 115), and Āqā Buzurg Ṭihrānī's *al-Dharīʿa* (22:272).

❖

3.3. Hadith

3.3.1 Miscellaneous

33. Al-Istibṣār fī-mā ikhtalaf min al-akhbār (A)

"The insight into disputed hadiths" is a well-known work by Ṭūsī which he mentions in his *al-Fihrist* (n.d., 161). It is also mentioned by Najāshī (1365 SH, 403) and Ibn Shahrāshūb (1380AH, 114). This is a major source of Shiite hadiths and one of the "Four Books" of the Shiʿa. It includes some hadiths from Ṭūsī's *Tahdhīb al-aḥkām* (Ṭūsī n.d., 161). It is structured in accordance with jurisprudential sections from cleanliness (*ṭahāra*) to blood money (*diyāt*). In each section, the author cites conflicting hadiths and then articulates ways of reconciling those hadiths. As Ṭūsī himself says, this is unprecedented in books by earlier scholars (Ṭūsī 1390 AH, 3). The book is organized into three parts: its first two volumes are devoted to worships, and its third volume is devoted to other sections of jurisprudence; that is, bilateral contracts (*'uqūd*), unilateral contracts (*īqā'āt*), to punishments (*ḥudūd*) and blood money (*diyāt*). The first volume contains 300 sections and 1899 hadiths; the second volume contains 217 sections and 1179 hadiths, and the third volume contains 398 sections and 2455 hadiths. Based on the author's own enumeration, it amounts to a total of 925 sections and 5511 hadiths. However, some people believe that this is a mistake as the accurate number of sections is 915 and that of hadiths is 5533 (Dirāyatī 1390 SH, 3:236). Since Ṭūsī did not mention the whole chain of transmitters for all hadiths in his *Tahdhīb al-aḥkām* and *al-Istibṣār*, he wrote a "mashīkha" (chain of masters) for both. Given the significance of this mashīkha, it has been frequently edited and annotated (Dirāyatī 1390 SH, 3:236).

Ṭūsī is explicit that he wrote this book after *Tahdhīb al-aḥkām* and *al-Nihāya* (1390 AH, 1:3; 4:305). The book has been published in four volumes.

The book is listed in Ṭūsī's own *al-Fihrist* (n.d., 161).

A manuscript of the book is available in the Library of Astan Quds Razavi in Mashhad, Iran (manuscript number: 31455). It was written in the tenth century AH (sixteenth century CE), but the scribe is unknown.

The book is critically edited and published in four volumes by Islāmiyya in Tehran in 1390 AH.

Many commentaries and glossaries have been written for *al-Istibṣār*, including:

1. *Mashīkhat al-tahdhīb wa-l-istibṣār* (The chain of masters of *al-Tahdhīb* and al-Istibṣār) by Ṭūsī.

2. *Taḥrīr bayān al-akhbār al-latī fī awwal al-istibṣār* (Editing the articulation of hadiths in the beginning of *al-Istibṣār*) or *Sharḥ muqaddimat al-istibṣār* (Exposition of *a-Istibṣār*'s preface) by Quṭb al-Dīn Rāwandī Sa'īd ibn Hibat Allāh) d. 573 AH/1177 CE).

3. *Istiqṣā' al-i'tibār fī sharḥ al-istibṣār* (Investigation of validity on exposition of al-Istibṣār) by Muḥammad ibn Ḥasan (980AH/1572CE - 1030 AH/1620 CE).

4. *Al-Fawā'id al-Makkiyya (Meccan points)*: commentaries on *al-Istibṣār* by Muḥammad Amīn ibn Muḥammad Sharīf Astarābādī (d. 1033 AH/1614 CE).

5. *Ḥāshiyat al-istibṣār* (Commentary on *al-Istibṣār*) by Mīr Dāmād Muḥammad Bāqir ibn Muḥammad (d. 1041 AH/1631 CE).

6. *Manāhij al-akhbār fī sharḥ kitāb al-istibṣār* (Methods of hadiths on exposition of the book *al-Istibṣār*) by Aḥmad ibn Zayn al-'Abidīn 'Alawī 'Āmilī) d. 1054 AH/1644 CE).

7. *Ḥāshiyat al-istibṣār* (Commentary on *al-Istibṣār*) by Muḥammad ibn Ḥasan Shīrwānī (1033 AH/1623 CE - 1098 AH/1686 CE).

8. *Ḥāshiyat al-istibṣār* (Commentary on *al-Istibṣār*) by Ḥusayn ibn Muḥammad Muḥaqqiq Khwānsārī (1016 AH/1607 CE - 1099 AH/1687 CE).

9. *Istibṣār al-akhbār* (The insight into hadiths) or *Jāmi' asrār al-'ulamā'* (Compendium of mysteries of the scholars) or *Jāmi' al-aḥādīth wa-l-aqwāl* (Compendium of hadiths and remarks) or *al-Jāmi' al-kabīr* (The great compendium) by Qāsim ibn Muḥammad ibn Rāwandī (d. 1100 AH/1688 CE).

10. *Kashf al-asrār fī sharḥ al-istibṣār* (Discovering the secrets in exposition of *al-Istibṣār*) by Niʿmat Allāh ibn ʿAbd Allāh Jazaʾirī (1050 AH/1640 CE - 1112 AH/1700 CE).

11. *Al-Iʿtibār fī ikhtiṣār al-istibṣār* (The validity in summary of *al-Istibṣār*) by Yaʿqūb ibn Ibrāhīm Bakhtiyārī Ḥuwayzī (d. 1150 AH/1737 CE).

12. *Sharḥ wa-tartīb mashīkha tahdhīb wa-istibṣār* (Exposition and organization of the chain of masters of *Tahdhīb* and *Istibṣār*) by Muḥammad Jaʿfar ibn Sayf al-Dīn Astarābādī (1198 AH/1783 CE - 1263 AH/1846 CE).

13. *Ḥadīqat al-anẓār fī mashīkhat al-faqīh wa-l-tahdhīb wa-l-istibṣār* (Garden of the eyes on the chain of masters of Al-faqīh and al-Tahdhīb and al-Istibṣār) by Muḥammad ʿAlī ibn Qāsim Ḥāʾirī.

14. *Jāmiʿ al-akhbār fī īḍāḥ al-istibṣār* (Compendium of hadiths in explication of *al-Istibṣār*) by Shaykh ʿAbd al-Laṭīf ibn ʿAlī ibn Aḥmad ibn Abī Jāmiʿ Ḥārithī Shāmī ʿĀmilī, a student of Shaykh Bahāʾī.

15. *Nukat al-irshād in sharḥ al-istibṣār* (Points of guidance on exposition of *al-Istibṣār*) by al-Shahīd al-Awwal Muḥammad ibn Makkī.

16. *Sharḥ al-istibṣār* (Exposition of *al-Istibṣār*) by Sayyid Mīrzā Ḥasan ibn ʿAbd al-Rasūl Ḥusaynī Zunnūzī Khūʾī (1172 AH/1758 CE - 1223 AH/1808 CE).

17. *Sharḥ al-istibṣār* (Exposition of al-Istibṣār) by Amīr Muḥammad ibn Amīr ʿAbd al-Wāsiʿ Khātūnābādī (ʿAllāma Majlisī's son in law; d. 1116 AH/1704 CE).

18. *Sharḥ al-istibṣār* (Exposition of *al-Istibṣār*) by Shaykh ʿAbd al-Riḍā Ṭufaylī Najafī.

19. *Sharḥ al-istibṣār* (Exposition of *al-Istibṣār*) by the jurist Qāsim ibn Muḥammad Jawād, known as Ibn Rāwandī and Faqīh Kāẓimī (d. after 1100 AH/1688 CE). He was contemporary with Ḥurr ʿĀmilī.

20. *Sharḥ al-istibṣār* (Exposition of *al-Istibṣār*) by Sayyid Muḥsin ibn Ḥasan Aʿrajī Kāẓimī (d. 1127 AH/1715 CE).

34. Al-Majālis fi l-akhbār (A)

"The meetings on hadiths" is a work by Ṭūsī, which he mentions with the above title in his *al-Fihrist* (n.d., 161). It is also mentioned by Ibn Shahrāshūb (1380 AH, 114). It is known as "al-Amālī" (The dictations) as well (Āqā Buzurg Ṭihrānī 1403 AH, 2:309). The book consists of meetings in which Ṭūsī dictated hadiths to his students. The meetings began in Baghdad, but a significant portion of them continued in Najaf until 458 AH/1065 CE (as pointed out by Ṭūsī in this book, 733). It is organized into eighteen parts and twenty-seven meetings. The eighteen parts preceding the meetings are widely believed to be dictations of Ṭūsī's son Abū ʿAlī (d. 515 AH/1121 CE), but the 27 meetings are dictations of Ṭūsī himself. However, Āqā Buzurg Ṭihrānī (1403 AH, 2:309) believes that the whole book—forty-five meetings—are dictated by Ṭūsī himself, but Abū ʿAlī dictated those eighteen parts after they were dictated by his father to his own students in 509 AH/1115 CE).

The hadiths in this book cover various topics, such as the principles of religion, virtues of the Infallibles (that is, Prophet Muḥammad and the Shiite Imams), history, ethics, and the like. The book has been published in 737 pages, including forty-six meetings.

The book is mentioned in the following classical bibliographies: Ṭūsī's *al-Fihrist* (n.d., 161), Ibn Shahrāshūb's *Maʿālim al-ʿulamāʾ* (1380 AH, 114), and Āqā Buzurg Ṭihrānī's *al-Dharīʿa* (1403 AH, 2:309).

A manuscript of the book is available in Markaz Iḥyā' in Qom, Iran (manuscript number: 3575). It is written in 313 pages by Yāsīn ibn Aḥmad ibn Muḥammad ibn Ibrāhīm known as Ṣarrāf on Thursday eve Dhu al-Qa?ʿdah 12, 982 AH (February 23, 1575 CE).

It has been critically edited and published by Dār al-Thiqāfa in Qom in 1414 AH.

35. Tahdhīb al-aḥkām (A)

"Refinement of the rulings" is a major book by Ṭūsī. It is mentioned by Ṭūsī in his own *al-Fihrist* (n.d., 161), Najāshī (1365 SH, 403), and Ibn Shahrāshūb (1380 AH, 114). This is one of the most important reliable sources of Shiite hadiths and one of the "Four Books" of the Shi?ʿa.

This is the first work written by Ṭūsī. It is an exposition of *al-Muqniʿa* by Mufīd (d. 413 AH/1022 CE) (Riḍādād and Ṭabāṭabā'ī 1387 SH, 56).

Ṭūsī began writing *Tahdhīb al-aḥkām* during the lifetime of his teacher Mufīd in 408 AH/1017 CE early after he arrived in Baghdad and finished the sections on cleanliness (*ṭahāra*) and prayer (*ṣalāt*) in 413 AH/1022 CE, but the book was not finished until 448 AH/1056 CE when he moved to Najaf (Āqā Buzurg Ṭihrānī 1403 AH, 4:504).

Tahdhīb al-aḥkām includes jurisprudential hadiths from cleanliness to blood money (*diyāt*). Ṭūsī sometimes explains hadiths and how to reconcile apparently conflicting ones. In writing the book, Ṭūsī consulted reliable primary principles (namely, early collections of hadiths compiled by their transmitters) many of which were written by transmitters of hadiths themselves (Mu'assasa Nūr 1391 AH, under *Tahdhīb al-aḥkām*). The book concludes with a "mashīkha" (chain of masters) in which Ṭūsī cites his chains of transmitters to the books and transmitters from whom he cites in *Tahdhīb al-aḥkām*. This is a significant piece in rijāl.

The book is organized into 393 sections, and the hadiths contained in it are said to be 13590 (Mu'assasa Nūr 1391 SH, under *Tahdhīb al-aḥkām*).

Āqā Buzurg saw the first part of the original manuscript of the book with Ṭūsī's own handwriting in a library in Tabriz (1403 AH, 4:504).

The book is mentioned in the following classical bibliographies: Ṭūsī's *al-Fihrist* (n.d., 161), Najāshī's *Rijāl* (1365 SH, 403), Ibn Shahrāshūb's *Maʿālim al-ʿulamā'* (1380 AH, 114), and Āqā Buzurg Ṭihrānī's *al-Dharīʿa* (1403 AH, 4:504).

A manuscript of the book is available in the Library of Sipahsālār School in Tehran, Iran (manuscript number: 3351). It is written in the ninth century AH (fifteenth century CE) in 422 pages, but the scribe is unknown. It is incomplete, covering the section on cleanliness (*ṭahāra*) through the section on jihad. Another manuscript is available in the Library of Astan Quds Razavi in Mashhad, Iran (manuscript number: 21183). It was written on Tuesday Muharram 3, 965 AH (October 26, 1557 CE) by Muḥammad ibn Aḥmad ibn Nāṣir al-Dīn Ḥusaynī in 250 pages. It is incomplete, covering the section on jihad through the section on marriage. A third manuscript is available in the Library of the Department of Theology at the University of Tehran (manuscript number: 244). It was written on Thursday eve, Rajab 12, 961 AH (June 13, 1554 CE) by Murtaḍā ibn Ḥusayn ibn Murtaḍā Ḥusaynī in 424 pages. It is incomplete, covering the part on the tradition from the section on marriage through the section on blood money (*diyāt*). Thus, taken together, these three manuscripts cover the whole book.

The book has been critically edited and published in ten volumes by Islāmiyya Publications in Tehran in 1365 SH.

Tahdhīb al-aḥkām has been translated into Persian by Muḥammad Yūsuf ibn Muḥammad Ibrāhīm Gūrkānī. It has also been translated into Persian by Muḥammad Taqī Gīlānī.

Many commentaries and glossaries have been written for *Tahdhīb al-aḥkām*, including:

1. *Mashīkhat al-tahdhīb wa-l-istibṣār* (The chain of masters of *al-Tahdhīb* and *al-Istibṣār*), by Ṭūsī. Commentaries have been written for this "mashīkha":

    a. Commentary by Sayyid Hāshim Tūblī Baḥrānī titled "Tanbīh al-arīb wa-tadhkirat al-labīb fī īḍāḥ rijāl al-tahdhīb" (Admonishment of the intellectual and reminder of the rational in clarification of hadith figures of *al-Tahdhīb*).

    b. Commentary by Ayatollah Burūjirdī titled "Tajrīd asānīd al-tahdhīb" (Abstraction of the chains of transmitters of *al-Tahdhīb*).

    c. "Sharḥ mashīkha tahdhīb al-aḥkām" (Exposition of the chain of masters of *Tahdhīb al-aḥkām*) by Sayyid Ḥasan Mūsawī Khursān.

    d. *Sharḥ wa-tartīb mashīkha tahdhīb wa istibṣār* (Exposition and organization of the chain of masters of *Tahdhīb* and *Istibṣār*) by Muḥammad Ja'far ibn Sayf al-Dīn Astarābādī (1198 AH/1783 CE - 1263 AH/1846 CE).

    e. *Ḥadīqat al-anẓār fī mashīkhat al-faqīh wa-l-tahdhīb wa-l-istibṣār* (Garden of the eyes in the chain of masters of *al-Faqīh* and *al-Tahdhīb* and *al-Istibṣār*) by Muḥammad 'Alī ibn Qāsim Ḥā'irī.

2. *Ḥāshiyat al-tahdhīb* (Commentary on *al-Tahdhīb*) by Ḥasan ibn Zayn al-Dīn 'Āmilī) 959 AH/1552 CE - 1011 AH/1602 CE).

3. *Ḥāshiya tahdhīb al-aḥkām* (Commentary on *Tahdhīb al-aḥkām*) by Muḥammad ibn Ḥasan ibn Zayn al-Dīn 'Āmilī.

4. *Sharḥ tahdhīb al-aḥkām* (Exposition of *Tahdhīb al-aḥkām*) by Muḥammad Amīn ibn Muḥammad Sharīf Astarābādī (d. 1033 AH/1614 CE).

5. *Iḥyā' al-aḥādīth fī sharḥ tahdhīb al-ḥadīth* (Revival of hadiths on exposition of the refinement of the hadith) by Muḥammad Taqī ibn Maqṣūd 'Alī Majlisī (1003 AH/1627 CE - 1070 AH/1699 CE).

6. *Fihrist tahdhīb al-aḥkām* (An index of *Tahdhīb al-aḥkām*) by 'Abd Allāh ibn Muḥammad Tūnī (d. 1071 AH/1660 CE).

7. *Mashāriq al-anwār fī sharḥ akhbār al-aʔimmat al-aṭhār* (Illumination of lights on exposition of hadiths from the pure Imams) by 'Abd Allāh ibn Muḥammad Taqī Majlisī (d. 1084 AH/1673 CE).

8. *Sharḥ tahdhīb al-aḥkām* (Exposition of *Tahdhīb al-aḥkām*) by Khalīl ibn Ghāzī Qazwīnī (1001 AH/1592 CE - 1089 AH/1678 CE).

9. *Ḥāshiya tahdhīb al-aḥkām* (Commentary on *Tahdhīb al-aḥkām*) by Muḥammad ibn Ḥasan Shīrwānī (1033 AH/1623 CE - 1098 AH/1686 CE).

10. *Ḥujjat al-islām fī sharḥ tahdhīb al-aḥkām* (Proof of Islam in exposition of *Tahdhīb al-aḥkām*) by Muḥammad Ṭāhir ibn Muḥammad Ḥusayn Qummī (d. 1098 AH/1686 CE).

11. *Fihrist tahdhīb al-aḥkām* (An index of *Tahdhīb al-aḥkām*) by 'Abd al-Kāfī Janābidhī.

12. *Ḥāshiya tahdhīb al-aḥkām* (Commentary on *Tahdhīb al-aḥkām*) by Muḥammad ibn Ḥasan Ḥurr 'Āmilī (1033 AH/1624 CE - 1104 AH/1693 CE).

13. *Tartīb al-tahdhīb* (Organizing *al-Tahdhīb*) or *Jāmiʿ al-aḥkām al-jisām fī aḥkām al-ḥalāl wa-l-ḥarām (Compendium of huge rulings on the rulings of the permitted and the forbidden)* by Hāshim ibn Sulaymān Baḥrānī (d. 1107 AH/1695 CE).

14. *Malādh al-akhyār fī fahm tahdhīb al-akhbār* (The refuge of good people in understanding the refinement of hadiths) by Muḥammad Bāqir ibn Muḥammad Taqī Majlisī (1037 AH/1627 CE - 1110 AH/1699 CE).

15. *Ḥāshiya tahdhīb al-aḥkām* (Commentary on *Tahdhīb al-aḥkām*) by Muḥammad Bāqir ibn Muḥammad Taqī Majlisī (1037 AH/1627 CE - 1110 AH/1699 CE).

16. *Ghāyat al-marām fī sharḥ tahdhīb al-aḥkām* (The ultimate purpose on exposition of *Tahdhīb al-aḥkām*) by Niʿmat Allāh ibn ʿAbd Allāh Jazāʾirī (1050 AH/1640 CE - 1112 AH/170 0CE).

17. *Kanz al-ṭālib wa-wasīlat al-rāghib* (The treasure of the seeker and the means of the interested) by Niʿmat Allāh ibn ʿAbd Allāh Jazāʾirī (1050 AH/1640 CE - 1112 AH/1700 CE).

18. *Maqṣūd al-anām fī sharḥ tahdhīb al-aḥkām* (The purpose of people in exposition of *Tahdhīb al-aḥkām*) by Niʿmat Allāh ibn ʿAbd Allāh Jazāʾirī (1050 AH/1640 CE - 1112 AH/1700 CE).

19. *Ḥāshiya tahdhīb al-aḥkām* (Commentary on *Tahdhīb al-aḥkām*) by Āqā Jamāl Khwānsārī (d. 1125 AH/1713 CE).

20. *Ḥāshiya tahdhīb al-aḥkām* (Commentary on *Tahdhīb al-aḥkām*) by Muḥammad Jaʿfar ibn Muḥammad Ṭāhir Khurāsānī (1080 AH/1669 CE - 1175 AH/1761 CE).

21. *Intikhāb al-jayyid min tanbīhāt al-sayyid* (Selection of the good from al-Sayyid's admonishments) by Ḥasan ibn Muḥammad Damistānī (d. 1191 AH/1777 CE).

22. *Man lā-yaḥḍuruh al-muḥaddith* (He who has no scholar of hadith in his presence) by Muḥammad ibn ʿAlī Shushtarī.

23. *Ḥawāshī tahdhīb al-aḥkām* (Commentaries on *Tahdhīb al-aḥkām*) by Shibr ibn Muḥammad Ḥusaynī Mūsawī.

24. *Tawḍīḥ al-marām fī sharḥ tahdhīb al-aḥkām* (Clarification of the purpose on exposition of *Tahdhīb al-aḥkām*) or *Tanqīḥ al-marām fī sharḥ tahdhīb al-aḥkām* (Refinement of the purpose in exposition of *Tahdhīb al-aḥkām*) by Muḥammad Naʿīm ibn Muḥammad Taqī ʿUrfī Ṭāliqānī.

25. *Fihrist tahdhīb al-aḥkām* (An index of *Tahdhīb al-aḥkām*) by Āqā Muḥammad ʿAlī Kirmānshāhī (1144 AH/1731 CE - 1216 AH/1801 CE).

26. *Fihrist tahdhīb al-aḥkām* (An index of *Tahdhīb al-aḥkām*) by Muḥammad Jaʿfar ibn Muḥammad Ṣafī Ābādi'ī (d. 1280 AH/1863 CE).

27. *Sharḥ tahdhīb al-aḥkām* (Exposition of *Tahdhīb al-aḥkām*) by Sayyid Muḥammad Mūsawī ʿĀmilī ,the author of *Madārik al-aḥkām* (d. 1009 AH/1600 CE).

28. *Tadhhīb al-akmām (Gilding the sleeves)* by Qāḍī Nūr Allāh Shahīd in 1019 AH/1610 CE.

29. *Sharḥ tahdhīb al-aḥkām* (Exposition of *Tahdhīb al-aḥkām*) by Mawlā ʿAbd Allāh Shushtarī (d. 1021 AH/1612 CE).

30. *Sharḥ tahdhīb al-aḥkām* (Exposition of *Tahdhīb al-aḥkām*) by Shaykh Muḥammad ibn Ḥasan ibn Shahīd Thānī (d. 1030 AH/1620 CE).
31. *Sharḥ tahdhīb al-aḥkām* (Exposition of Tahdhīb al-aḥkām) by Muḥammad Amīn Astarābādī (d. 1036 AH/1614 CE).
32. *Sharḥ tahdhīb al-aḥkām* (Exposition of Tahdhīb al-aḥkām) by ʿAbd al-Laṭīf Jāmiʿī) d. 1050 AH/1640 CE), a student of Shaykh Bahāʾī.
33. *Ḥāshiya tahdhīb al-aḥkām* (Commentary on Tahdhīb al-aḥkām) by Waḥīd Bihbahānī (d. 1205 AH/1791 CE).
34. *Ḥāshiya tahdhīb al-aḥkām* (Commentary on *Tahdhīb al-aḥkām*) by Mīrzā ʿAbd Allāh Afandī (d. 1130 AH/1718 CE), the author of *Riyāḍ al-aḥkām*.
35. *Ḥāshiya tahdhīb al-aḥkām* (Commentary on *Tahdhīb al-aḥkām*) by Shaykh Muḥammad ʿAlī Balāghī (d. 1352A H/1933 CE).

❖

3.4. Rijāl

36. Ikhtiyār al-rijāl (A)

"Selection of hadith figures" is a work by Ṭūsī concerning *rijāl* (study of the reliability of transmitters of hadiths). It is mentioned by Ṭūsī in his own *Al-fihrist* (n.d., 161) and Ibn Shahrāshūb (1380AH, 115). It is known as "Ikhtiyār maʿrifat al-rijāl" (Selection of knowledge of hadith figures) as well (Adībīmihr 1384 SH, 132).

This is in fact, Kashshī's well-known book of *rijāl* called *Maʿrifat al-nāqilīn ʿan al-aʾimmat al-ṣādiqīn* (Knowledge of narrators from the truthful Imams) as edited and refined by Ṭūsī as it contained many errors (Āqā Buzurg Ṭihrānī 1403 AH, 1:366). Since Kashshī's book of *rijāl* has been lost, what is available today is, in fact, Ṭūsī's edition of the book (Dirāyatī 1390 SH, 2:461).

The book begins with Prophet Muḥammad's companions (*Ṣaḥāba*) and then proceeds to evaluate companions Shiite Imams by reports in their praise or blame. Transmitters of hadiths are mentioned in the chronological, rather than alphabetic, order.

The book is listed in the following classical bibliographies: Ṭūsī's own *al-Fihrist* (n.d., 161), Ibn Shahrāshūb's *Ma'ālim al-'ulamā'* (1380 AH, 115), and Āqā Buzurg Ṭihrānī's *al-Dharī'a* (1403 AH, 1:366).

A manuscript of the book is available in Malik Library in Tehran, Iran (manuscript number: 3589). It was written on Jumada al-Thani 10, 964 AH (April 10, 1557 CE) in 173 pages, but the scribe is unknown.

Ṭūsī's *Ikhtiyār al-rijāl* has been critically edited and published by Markaz Nashr Āthār 'Allāma Muṣṭafawī in 1388 SH.

The book has been reorganized into various orders (*tartīb*), including:

1. The order of Sayyid Yūsuf ibn Muḥammad Ḥusaynī 'Āmilī) died in the tenth century AH/ sixteenth century CE.(
2. The order of Muḥammad ibn Ḥisām al-Dīn Jazā'irī Mushrifī (d. after 1042 AH/1632 CE).
3. The order of Ḥisām al-Dīn Jazā'irī (died in the eleventh century AH/ seventeenth century CE).
4. The order of 'Ināyat Allāh Quhpāyī (died in the eleventh century AH/ seventeenth century CE).
5. The order of Dāwūd ibn Ḥasan Baḥrānī (died in the twelfth century AH/ eighteenth century CE).

Commentaries and glossaries have also been written for the book, including:

1. Commentary by Mīr Muḥammad Bāqir Astarābādī, known as Mīr Dāmād (d. 1041 AH/1631 CE).
2. Commentary by ʿInāyat Allāh Quhpāyī (died in the eleventh century AH/ seventeenth century CE).

37. Rijāl al-Ṭūsī (A)

"Ṭūsī's men of hadith figures" is a work in *rijāl* by Ṭūsī. Its full title in Ṭūsī's own *al-Fihrist* (n.d., 160) is "Al-rijāl al-ladhīn rawaw ʿan al-nabī wa-l-aʾimmat al-ithnā ʿashar ʿalayhim al-salām wa-man taʾakhkhar ʿanhim" (The figures who transmitted hadiths from the Prophet and the Twelve Imams, peace be upon them, and those who came after them). It is known as "Kitāb al-rijāl" (Book of hadith figures), "Al-rijāl man rawā ʿan al-nabī wa-ʿan al-aʾimma" (The figures who transmitted hadiths from the Prophet and the Imams), and "Kitāb al-abwāb" (Book of sections) as well (Ibn Shahrāshūb 1380 AH, 115; Najāshī 1365 SH, 403; Āqā Buzurg Ṭihrānī 1403 AH, 1:73).

In this book, Ṭūsī has compiled and enumerated the names of the companions of Prophet Muḥammad and Shiite Imams, without engaging in an assessment of their reliability or unreliability in the transmission of hadiths except in certain cases (Mu'assasa Nūr 1391 SH, under *Rijāl al-Ṭūsī*).

As he himself points out, Ṭūsī wrote the book at the request of a learned scholar, but he does not mention him by name. Probably this scholar was Qāḍī Ibn Barrāj (d. 481 AH/1088 CE), at the request of whom Ṭūsī wrote other books as well (Dirāyatī 1390 SH, 16:285). Some researchers date the writing of the book back to Sayyid Murtaḍā's lifetime; that is, before 436 AH/1044 CE, because of certain phrases it contains about him, which signify that he was alive when the book was being written. But others believe that the book was written toward the end of Ṭūsī's life since it involves reference to his *al-Fihrist* (Mu'assasa Nūr 1391 SH, under *Rijāl al-Ṭūsī*).

The book has been published in 452 pages.

Rijāl al-Ṭūsī has been listed in the following classical bibliographies: Ṭūsī's *al-Fihrist* (n.d., 160), Najāshī's *Rijāl* (1365 SH, 403), Ibn Shahrāshūb's *Ma'ālim al-'ulamā'* (1380 AH, 115), and Āqā Buzurg Ṭihrānī's *al-Dharī'a* (1403 AH, 1:73).

A photographed manuscript of the book is available in Markaz Iḥyā' in Qom, Iran (manuscript number: 589). The original version of this manuscript is held in British Museum in London, UK. Another photographed manuscript is available in Markaz Iḥyā' in Qom, Iran (manuscript number 2256). The original version of this is available in the Library of Kāshif al-Ghiṭā' in Najaf, Iraq. It was written in 144 pages on Jumada al-Awwal 16, 973 AH (December 9, 1565 CE) by 'Alī ibn Idrīs.

Rijāl al-Ṭūsī has been critically edited and published by Jāmi'i Mudarrisīn in Qom in 1415 AH.

The book has been reorganized into a new order by Muḥammad Ḥusayn Ṭabāṭabā'ī Burūjirdī (1253 AH/1875 CE - 1340 AH/1961 CE).

38. Al-Fihrist (A)

"The list" with the full title: "Fihrist kutub al-Shī'a wa-uṣūlihim wa-asmā**?**' al-muṣannifīn minhum wa-aṣḥāb al-uṣūl" [The list of books by the Shi'a and their principles and the names of their authors and holders of principles] (Ibn Shahrāshūb 1380 AH, 115), and "...wa-l-kutub wa-asmā' man ṣannaf lahum wa-lays huwa minhum" [...and books and the names of those who wrote for them but did not belong to them] (Ṭūsī, *al-Fihrist*, n.d., 160). This is a bibliography in which Ṭūsī mentions about 900 authors and their works, pointing to the views of scholars concerning their reliability. He also transmits chains of transmitters from his own teachers. This is one of the "four principles of rijāl" (Āqā Buzurg Ṭihrānī, *al-Dharī'a*, 1403 AH, 16/385), and some contemporary researchers refer to it as the first major Shiite book of *rijāl* (Adībīmihr 1384 AH, 134). It seems that Ṭūsī wrote part of the book during the lifetime of Sayyid Murtaḍā (d. 436 AH/1044 CE) and another part of it after his death (Riḍādād and Ṭabāṭabā'ī 1387 AH, 60).

The book is mentioned in the following classical bibliographies: Ṭūsī's *al-Fihrist* (n.d., 160), Ibn Shahrāshūb's *Ma'ālim al-*'**ulamā**' (1380AH/115), and Āqā Buzurg Ṭihrānī's *al-Dharī'a* (1403 AH, 16:385).

A manuscript of the book is available at the Library of the Department of Literature in the University of Tehran (manuscript number: 213/1). It was written in 66 pages in eighth-ninth centuries AH (fourteenth and fifteenth centuries CE) by Zayn al-Dīn ibn '**Alī** ibn Aḥmad '**Āmilī, as permitted by Shahīd Thānī in Dhu al-Hajjah 953 (January 1547).**

Al-Fihrist was critically edited and published in 381 pages by Fiqāhat Publications in Qom in 1429 AH.

The following are commentaries on and summaries of *al-Fihrist*:

1. *Talkhīṣ al-fihrist li-l-Ṭūsī* (Summary of Ṭūsī's *al-Fihrist*) by Muḥaqqiq Ḥillī (602 AH/1205 CE - 676 AH/1277 CE).

2. *Mi'rāj al-kamāl ilā ma'rifat al-rijāl* (Ascent of perfection to the knowledge of figures) by Sulaymān ibn '**Abd** Allāh Baḥrānī (1075 AH/1664 CE - 1121 AH/1709 CE).

3. *Tartīb al-fihrist li-l-Ṭūsī* (Reorganization of Ṭūsī's *al-Fihrist*) by 'Ināyat Allāh ibn '**Alī** Quhpā'**ī** (eleventh century AH/seventeenth century CE).

4. *Talkhīṣ al-fihrist li-l-Ṭūsī* (Summary of Ṭūsī's *al-Fihrist*) by '**Abd** al-Ghafūr ibn '**Abd** al-Nabī Anṣārī Lārī (thirteenth century AH/nineteenth century CE).

3.5. Quranic Sciences

3.5.1. Quranic Exegesis

39. Al-Tibyān fī tafsīr al-Qur'ān (A)

"The clarification in the exegesis of the Quran" is a well-known exegesis of the Quran by Ṭūsī. It is mentioned in some versions of *al-Fihrist* (1420 AH, 450). It is mentioned with the above title by Najāshī (1365 SH, 403) and Ibn Shahrāshūb (1380 AH, 115) as well. It is known as "al-Tibyān al-Jāmi' li-'ulūm al-Qur'ān" (The comprehensive clarification of Quran's sciences) as well (Dirāyatī 1390 SH, 6:896; Āqā Buzurg Ṭihrānī 1403 AH, 3:328).

This is the first complete Shiite exegesis of the Quranو which draws on relevant sciences and techniques such as Arabic morphology and syntax, lexical derivation, rhetoric, hadith, jurisprudence, theology, and history. Before this, Shiite exegetes rested content with citation of hadiths from Shiite Imams or their companions or occasional references to certain lexicological points (Mu'assasa Nūr 1391 SH, under *al-Tibyān fī tafsīr al-Qur'ān*).

Ṭūsī wrote this exegesis during his time in Baghdad after Sayyid Murtaḍā's death in 436 AH/1044 CE (Riḍādād and Ṭabāṭabā'ī 1387 SH, 63). It has been said that the writing of the book was finished in Rajab 441AH (December 1049 CE) (Dirāyatī 1390 SH, 6:896).

The book has been published in ten volumes.

Al-Tibyān fī tafsīr al-Qur'ān is listed in the following classical bibliographies: Ṭūsī's own *al-Fihrist* (1420 AH, 450), Najāshī's *Rijāl* (1365 SH, 403), Ibn Shahrāshūb's *Ma'ālim al-'ulamā'* (1380 AH, 115), and Āqā Buzurg Ṭihrānī's *al-Dharī'a* (1403 AH, 3:328-30).

All available manuscripts of the book are incomplete; for example, a photographed manuscript in the Library of Ayatollah Mar'ashī Najafī (numbers 83 and 76). It was written in the fifth century AH (eleventh century CE), covering the Qurān 3:121 through 4:50.

The book has been critically edited and published by Dār Iḥyā' al-Turāth al-'Arabī in Beirut.

A selection of the book has been written by Muḥammad ibn Aḥmad ibn Idrīs (543 AH/1148 CE - 598 AH/1201 CE) under *Al-Muntakhab min tafsīr al-Qur'ān* (The selection from the exegesis of the Quran) and *al-Nukat al-mustakhraja min kitāb al-tibyān* (Extracted points from the book *al-Tibyān*).

3.5.2. Missing Works

40. Al-Masā'il al-rajabiyya fī tafsīr al-Qur'ān (C)

"Rajabi questions in the exegesis of the Qur'an" is a work by Ṭūsī, which he mentions in his *al-Fihrist* (n.d., 161), commenting that it is unique. In some other versions of *al-Fihrist* (1420 AH, 450) as well as in *al-Dharī'a* (1403 AH, 20:348), it is titled "al-Masā'il al-rajabiyya fī tafsīr āy min al-Qur'ān" (Rajabi questions in the exegesis of a verse from the Quran).

As the title suggests, it is an essay in Quranic exegesis. No manuscript of the work is available.

It is mentioned in the following classical bibliographies: Ṭūsī's *al-Fihrist* (n.d., 161; 1420 AH, 450) and Āqā Buzurg Ṭihrānī's *al-Dharīʿa* (1403 AH, 20:348).

41. Al-Masāʾil al-Dimashqiyya (C)

"Questions from Damascus" is a work by Ṭūsī, which he mentions in his *al-Fihrist* (n.d., 161). It is noted in *al-Dharīʿa* under "Jawābāt al-masāʾil al-Dimashqiyya" (Replies to questions from Damascus) as well (1403 AH, 5:220). The essay includes twelve questions. Given a manuscript of *al-Fihrist* was available to Āqā Buzurg Ṭihrānī, he says that the questions were concerned with Quranic exegesis: "he [Ṭūsī] said in *al-Fihrist* that these were twelve questions in Quranic exegesis, the like of which was not done" (1403 AH, 20:347). But in versions of *al-Fihrist* available to us, no comment is made on this title (Ṭūsī n.d., 161; 1420 AH, 450).

The essay is mentioned in the following classical bibliographies: Ṭūsī's *al-Fihrist* (n.d., 161) and Āqā Buzurg Ṭihrānī's *al-Dharīʿa* (1403 AH, 5:220; 20:347).

❖

3.6. Principles of Jurisprudence

3.6.1 Miscellaneous

42. Al-ʿUdda fī uṣūl al-fiqh (A)

"The preparation in the principles of jurisprudence" is a work by Ṭūsī, which he mentions in his *al-Fihrist* (n.d., 160), and is also mentioned by Najāshī (1365 SH, 403) and Ibn Shahrāshūb (1380 AH, 115). It is referred to as "'Uddat al-uṣūl" (Preparation of the principles) as well (Adībīmihr 1384 SH, 138).

This is an essay in principles of jurisprudence, encompassing all the issues discussed at the time. He wrote the work at the request of some of his students or scholars, as he points out in the opening of this book (1417 AH, 1:3). After *al-Dharī'a* by Sayyid Murtaḍā (d. 436 AH/1044 CE), this is the oldest work in Shiite principles of jurisprudence (Dirāyatī 1390 SH, 22:463). The book includes an introduction, two parts, and twelve sections. In this book, Ṭūsī introduces the theories of Sunni scholars in addition to those of Shiite scholars.

According to some researchers, the book was being written simultaneously with *Talkhīṣ al-shāfī* about 432 AH/1040 CE. There is evidence that part of it was written during the lifetime of Sayyid Murtaḍā (before 436 AH/1044 CE) and part of it was written after his death (Riḍādād and Ṭabāṭabā'ī 1387 SH, 57-8).

The book has been published in two volumes.

Al-'Udda fī uṣūl al-fiqh is listed in the following classical bibliographies: Ṭūsī's *al-Fihrist* (n.d., 160), Najāshī's *Rijāl* (1365SH, 403), Ibn Shahrāshūb's *Ma'ālim al-'ulamā'* (1380 AH, 115), and Āqā Buzurg Ṭihrānī's *al-Dharī'a* (1403 AH, 15:227).

A manuscript of the book is available in the Library of Astan Quds Razavi in Mashhad, Iran (manuscript number: 2916). It was written in 205 pages in Dhu al-Hijjah 518 AH (January 1125 CE) by 'Abd al-Ṣamad ibn 'Abd Allāh ibn Ḥusayn ibn Aḥmad.

The book has been critically edited and published in two volumes by Sitāra Publications in Qom in 1417 AH.

Commentaries and expositions have been written for *al-'Udda fī uṣūl al-fiqh*, including:

1. *Ḥāshiya ʻuddat al-uṣūl* (Commentary on *ʻUddat al-uṣūl*) by Khalīl ibn Ghāzī Qazwīnī (1001 AH/1592 CE - 1089 AH/1678 CE).

2. Jabr wa-ikhiyār (Determinism and free will), an exposition of part of *ʻUddat al-uṣūl* by Muḥammad Bāqir ibn Ḥāfiẓ Kanjī Bayk Tabrīzī (the twelfth century AH/ eighteenth century CE).

3. *Najāt al-muslimīn wa-munjī al-hālikīn* (Salvation of Muslims and rescuer of those who perish) by Muḥammad Mahdī ibn Muḥammad Bāqir Ḥusaynī Mashhadī (the twelfth century AH/ eighteenth century CE).

4. *Tanqīḥ al-marām fī ḥāshiya sharḥ ʻuddat al-uṣūl* (Refinement of the purpose in commentary on exposition of *ʻUddat al-uṣūl*) by ʻAlī Aṣghar ibn Muḥammad Yūsuf Qazwīnī (d. 1120 AH/1708 CE).

5. *Ḥāshiya sharḥ ʻuddat al-uṣūl* (Commentary on the exposition of *ʻUddat al-uṣūl*) by ʻAlī Aṣghar ibn Muḥammad Yūsuf Qazwīnī (d. 1120 AH/1708 CE).

6. *Ḥāshiya ḥāshiya ʻuddat al-uṣūl* (Commentary on a commentary on *ʻUddat al-ūsūl*) by Muḥammad Bāqir ibn Ghāzī Qazwīnī (thirteenth century AH/ nineteenth century CE).

7. *Sharḥ ʻuddat al-uṣūl* (Exposition of *ʻUddat al-uṣūl*) by Muḥammad ibn Muḥammad Ṣādiq Ḥusaynī Qazwīnī (thirteenth century AH/ nineteenth century CE).

8. *Tuḥaf al-ʻuqūl fī sharḥ ʻuddat al-uṣūl* (Gifts of reasons in exposition of *ʻUddat al-uṣūl)* by Khiḍr ibn Ismāʻīl Ashrafī Māzandarānī (d. 1336 AH/1917 CE).

3.6.2. Missing Works

43. Sharḥ al-sharḥ fi l-uṣūl (C)

"Exposition of the exposition in principles" is a work by Ṭūsī. This was apparently an exposition of Sayyid Murtaḍā's "Sharḥ jumal al-ʿilm wa-l-ʿamal" (Exposition of the statements of knowledge and act" or "Tamhīd al-uṣūl" (Preparation of the principles). Āqā Buzurg Ṭihrānī believes that this is distinct from that book (1403 AH, 2:198), and Ṭūsī does not mention it in his *al-Fihrist*. Ḥasan Salīqī, a student of Ṭūsī, said: "this is an elaborate book a bulk of which he [Ṭūsī] dictated to us, but he died before he finished it" (see Ṭihrānī 1403 AH, 13:332; also see Ṭihrānī 1376 SH). Some researchers believe that *Sharḥ al-Sharḥ* is the same as *Uṣūl al-ʿaqāʾid* or *Sharḥ al-tamhīd fi l-uṣūl* (Wāʿiẓzāda, 1:69). However, other researchers believe appeal to this remark by Salīqī to show that these are distinct (Adībīmihr 1384 SH, 137). Given Salīqī's remarks that Ṭūsī died before finishing this work, this might be believed to be the last work by Ṭūsī (Riḍādād and Ṭabāṭabāʾī 1387 SH, 68).

Of classical bibliographies, the work is only mentioned in Āqā Buzurg Ṭihrānī's *al-Dharīʿa* (1403 AH, 2:198, 13:332).

44. Masʾala fi l-ʿamal bi-khabar al-wāḥid (C)

"A problem about acting upon single-narrator reports" is a work by Ṭūsī, which he mentions in his *al-Fihrist* (n.d., 161). It is also mentioned by Najāshī (1365 SH, 403). In some sources, it is referred to as "Ḥujjiyyat al-akhbār" (Reliability of reports) as well (Āqā Buzurg Ṭihrānī 1403 AH, 6:270). This is an essay of principles of jurisprudence dealing with the reliability of "khabar al-wāḥid" or single-narrator reports.

Since Najāshī has mentioned the essay, it must have been written before his death in 450 AH (1058 CE). No manuscript of the essay has been found.

The work is mentioned in the following classical bibliographies: Ṭūsī's *al-Fihrist* (n.d., 161), Najāshī's *Rijāl* (1365 SH, 403), and Āqā Buzurg Ṭihrānī's *al-Dharī'a* (1403 AH, 6:270).

❖

3.7. Supplications

45. Mukhtaṣar al-miṣbāḥ fī 'amal al-sunna (A)

"The summary of the lamp in acts of tradition" is a work by Ṭūsī concerning supplications, which he mentions in his *al-Fihrist* (n.d., 161). It is known as "al-Miṣbāḥ al-ṣaghīr" (The small lamp), "'Amal al-sunna" (Act of the tradition), and "Mukhtaṣar al-miṣbāḥ" (Summary of the lamp) as well (Adībīmihr 1384 SH, 140; Dirāyatī 1390 AH, 28:618).

This is a summary of another book of supplications by Ṭūsī, *Miṣbāḥ al-mutahajjid* (The vigilant's lamp). It is concerned with rulings, supplications, and worships. The book has been published in 786 pages.

Mukhtār al-miṣbāḥ is listed in the following classical bibliographies: Ṭūsī's *al-Fihrist* (n.d., 161) and Āqā Buzurg Ṭihrānī's *al-Dharī'a* (1403 AH, 21/118).

A manuscript of the book is available in the Library of Ayatollah Mar'ashī Najafī (manuscript number: 13056). It was written in 176 pages by an unknown scribe in the first half of the sixth century AH (twelfth century CE).

Mukhtār al-miṣbāḥ is critically edited by Muḥammad Jawād Sha'bānī and Muḥammad Ḥasan Āmūzgār and published in Qom by Maktabat al-'Allāma al-Majlisī in 1435AH.

46. Miṣbāḥ al-mutahajjid fī 'amal al-sunnā (A)

"The vigilant's lamp in the act of the tradition" is a work of supplications by Ṭūsī, which is mentioned by Ṭūsī in his *al-Fihrist* (n.d., 161) and Ibn Shahrāshūb (1380 AH, 115). It is known as "A'māl al-sunna" (Acts of the tradition), "Miṣbāḥ al-mutahajjid" (The vigilant's lamp), and "Silāḥ al-muta'abbid" (The worshipper's weapon) as well (Adībīmihr 1384 SH, 145). Ṭūsī introduces certain rulings of ritual cleanliness, prayer, and zakat, and then mentions supererogatory acts, supplications, and worships. It has been published in two volumes. This is one of the most reliable books of supplications and worships, which served as a source for later supplication books by Shiite scholars (Mu'assasa Nūr 1391 SH, under *Miṣbāḥ al-mutahajjid*). It was written in the years before Ṭūsī's migration from Baghdad to Najaf in 448 AH/1056 CE (Riḍādād and Ṭabāṭabā'ī 1387 SH, 65; Dirāyatī 1390 SH, 29:806).

Ṭūsī himself summarized the book as "Mukhtaṣar al-miṣbāḥ" (Summary of the lamp).

Miṣbāḥ al-mutahajjid is mentioned in the following classical bibliographies: Ṭūsī's *al-Fihrist* (n.d., 161), Ibn Shahrāshūb's *Ma'ālim al-'ulamā'* (1380 AH, 115), and Āqā Buzurg Ṭihrānī's *al-Dharī'a* (1403 AH, 21:118).

A manuscript of the book is available in the Library of Astan Quds Razavi in Mashhad, Iran (manuscript number: 8822). It has been transcribed in 208 pages by 'Abd al-Jabbār ibn 'Alī ibn Manṣūr al-Taffāsh al-Rāzī in Mashhad from a contemporary manuscript written by Shaykh Abū Isḥāq Ibrāhīm ibn Muḥammad Māwarā? ' al-Nahrī. 'Abd al-Jabbār finished the transcription of this manuscript on Thursday, Safar 23, 502 AH (October 2, 1108 CE).

Miṣbāḥ al-mutahajjid has been critically edited and published in two volumes by Muʾassasa Fiqh Shīʿa in Beirut in 1411 AH.

Many expositions, summaries, and commentaries have been written for the book, including:

1. *Mukhtaṣar miṣbāḥ al-mutahajjid* (Summary of *Miṣbāḥ al-mutahajjid*) by Ṭūsī himself.
2. *Qabas al-miṣbāḥ* (Fire of the lamp): a selection of *Miṣbāḥ al-mutahajjid* by Sulaymān ibn Ḥasan Ṣahrashtī (fifth century AH/ eleventh century CE).
3. *Jamāl al-usbūʿ bi-kamāl al-ʿamal al-mashrūʿ* (Beauty of the week by the accomplishment of the legitimate act) by ʿAlī ibn Mūsā ibn Ṭāwūs (589 AH/1193 CE - 664 AH /1266 CE). This work has been translated into Persian by Muḥammad Ḥusayn ibn Riḍwān (eleventh century AH/seventeenth century CE).
4. *Al-Ikhtiyār min al-miṣbāḥ* (The selection from *al-Miṣbāḥ*) by ʿAlī ibn Ḥusayn al-Bāqī (seventh century AH/thirteenth century CE).
5. *Minhāj al-ṣalāḥ fī ikhtiṣār al-miṣbāḥ* (Way of improvement in the summary of *al-Miṣbāḥ*) by ʿAllāma Ḥillī (684 AH/1250 CE - 726 AH/1325 CE).
6. *Īḍāḥ al-miṣbāḥ li-ahl al-ṣalāḥ)Clarification of* Al-miṣbāḥ *for people of improvement)* by ʿAlī ibn ʿAbd al-Karīm Nassāba (d. 800 AH/1397 CE).
7. *Mukhtaṣar miṣbāḥ al-mutahajjid (Summary of* Miṣbāḥ al-mutahajjid*)* by Ḥaydar ʿAlī ibn Muḥammad Shīrwānī (twelfth century AH/eighteenth century CE).

The book has also been translated into Persian by Muḥammad Ḥusayn ibn ʿAbd al-Ḥusayn under *Ikhtiyār al-miṣbāḥ* (Selection of *al-Miṣbāḥ*) and by Ghiyāth al-Dīn ibn Jamāl al-Dīn Wāʿiẓ.

3.7.1. Missing Works

47. Hidāyat al-mustarshid wa-baṣīrat al-mutaʿabbid (C)

"The guide-seeking's guide and the worshipper's insight" is a work by Ṭūsī, which is mentioned by Ṭūsī himself in his *al-Fihrist* (n.d., 161) and by Ibn Shahrāshūb (1380 AH, 115). This essay concerns supplications (Āqā Buzurg 1376 SH, 64). In his *Fatḥ al-abwāb* (Opening of the gates), Ibn Ṭāwūs quotes texts from this work concerning "istikhāra" (seeking guidance from God on a specific action) (Ibn Ṭāwūs 1409 AH, 177, 242). No manuscript of the book is available today, but it seems to have been available in Majlisī's time because it appears on his permission in 599 AH/1202 CE (Majlisī 1403 AH, 106:39). The book was probably written after Najāshī's death in 450 AH/1058 CE because it does not appear on his *Rijāl* (Riḍādād and Ṭabāṭabāʾī 1387SH, 67).

Hidāyat al-mustarshid is listed in the following classical bibliographies: Ṭūsī's *al-Fihrist* (n.d., 161) and Ibn Shahrāshūb (1380 AH, 115).

❖

3.8. Others

48. Sharāʾiṭ dīn al-Imāmiyya (A)

"Conditions of the Imāmī religion" is a work that does not appear in none of the bibliographies and biographies. There is a manuscript with this title in the Library of the University of Tehran, which begins with "From the dictation of Shaykh Abī Ja'far Ṭūsī" which implies its attribution to Ṭūsī. As the title suggests, this is an essay concerning the principles of beliefs.

The work's manuscript is available in the Library of the University of Tehran (manuscript number: 3514/16). The scribe and the date of transcription are not known.

49. Ṣalawāt (A)

"Greetings" is a work cited in the list of manuscripts of the Library of the University of Tehran, without further information available. Given our methodology, its attribution to Ṭūsī is not doubtful because it has not been called into question by any researcher, although evidence for its attribution is not compelling.

The manuscript available in the University of Tehran (manuscript number: 1258/2) has no date, and the scribe is unknown.

50. Al-Sharq wa-l-barq (A)

"Illumination and lighting" is only mentioned in the list of manuscripts in the Vaziri Library. Given our methodology, its attribution to Ṭūsī is not doubtful because it has not been called into question by any researcher, although evidence for its attribution is not compelling.

A manuscript of the work is available in Vaziri Library in Yazd, Iran (manuscript number: 2297/1). It was transcribed in the thirteenth century AH (nineteenth century CE), but the scribe is unknown.

51. Majmūʿa (A)

"The collection" is only mentioned in the list of manuscripts in the Vaziri Library. Given the manuscript's opening, it includes eleven books and a set of jurisprudential problems. According to our methodology, its attribution to Ṭūsī is not doubtful because it has not been called into question by any researcher, although evidence for its attribution is not compelling.

The manuscript is available in Vaziri Library in Yazd, Iran (manuscript number: 1008). It was transcribed in 193 pages in 1239 AH/1823 CE by Abu l-Ḥasan ibn Muṭṭalib Ardakānī.

52. Makārim al-akhlāq (A)

"The honored moralities" is only mentioned in the list of manuscripts in the Library of Astan Quds Razavi in Mashhad. As suggested by its title, it is probably concerned with morality. Given our methodology, its attribution to Ṭūsī is not doubtful because it has not been called into question by any researcher, although evidence for its attribution is not compelling.

The manuscript is available in the Library of Astan Quds Razavi in Mashhad, Iran (manuscript number: 17822). The date and the scribe of the manuscript are not known.

3.8.1. Missing Works

53. Al-Masā?'il al-Qummiyya (C)

"Questions from Qom" is a work which Āqā Buzurg Ṭihrānī (1403) has seen in certain manuscripts of Ṭūsī's *al-Fihrist*, although it is not found in versions of *al-Fihrist* available to us. The essay is also mentioned by

Ibn Shahrāshūb (1380 AH, 115). The essay seems to consist in answers to certain questions, but the subject-matter of the questions and replies is not known (Wā'iẓzāda 1363 SH, 43). No manuscript of the essay is available.

The essay is listed in the following classical bibliographies: Ibn Shahrāshūb's *Ma'ālim al-'ulamā'* 1380 AH, 115 and Āqā Buzurg Ṭihrānī's *al-Dharī'a* (1403 AH).

54. Uns al-waḥīd (C)

"Companionship of the lonely" is a work mentioned by Ṭūsī himself in his *al-Fihrist* (n.d., 161) and by Ibn Shahrāshūb (1380 AH, 115). In some sources, it is mentioned as "Uns al-tawḥīd" (Companionship of monotheism) as well (Adībīmihr 1384 AH, 133).

It is unknown what this work is concerned with, although some people have speculated that it is a work of supplications or an anthology (Wā'iẓzāda 1363 SH, 43). The word "Majmū?'" (collection), which Ṭūsī mentions immediately after he mentions the work, supports the thesis that the work is an anthology (Adībīmihr 1384 SH, 133). No manuscript of the work is available.

Since the work is not mentioned by Najāshī (d. 450 AH/1058 CE) and is mentioned toward the end of Ṭūsī's *al-Fihrist*, it has been speculated that it was written after Najāshī's death; that is, the last decade of Ṭūsī's life (Riḍādād and Ṭabāṭabā'ī 1387 SH, 67).

The work is mentioned in the following classical bibliographies: Ṭūsī's *al-Fihrist* (n.d., 161), Ibn Shahrāshūb's *Ma'ālim al-'ulamā'* (1380 AH, 115), and Āqā Buzurg Ṭihrānī's *al-Dharī'a* (1403 AH, 2:368).

55. Mas'ala fi l-aḥwāl (C)

"A question about the states" is a work mentioned by Ṭūsī in his own *al-Fihrist* (n.d., 161), Najāshī (1365 SH, 404), and Ibn Shahrāshūb (1380 AH, 115). Some contemporary researchers have referred to the work as "Mas?'ala fi l-uṣūl" (A question about the principles) (Wāʿiẓzāda 1363 SH, 43), which might be derived from some other source (Adībīmihr 1384 SH, 141). Since Najāshī mentions the work, it must have been written during his lifetime, before 450 AH/1058 CE.

No manuscript of the work has so far been found, and no comment on its content has been made by any bibliography or biography.

The work is listed in the following classical bibliographies: Ṭūsī's *al-Fihrist* (n.d., 161), Najāshī's *Rijāl* (1365 SH, 404), Ibn Shahrāshūb's *Ma'ālim al-ʿulamā'* (1380 AH, 115), and Āqā Buzurg Ṭihrānī's *al-Dharīʿa* (1403 AH, 20:382).

56. Al-Masā'il al-Ilyāsiyya (C)

"Questions from Ilyās" is a work mentioned by Ṭūsī in his own *al-Fihrist* (n.d., 161) and by Ibn Shahrāshūb (1380 AH, 115). It is referred to as "Jawābāt al-masā'il al-Ilyāsiyya" (Replies to questions from Ilyās) as well (Āqā Buzurg Ṭihrānī 1403 AH). As Ṭūsī himself points out (n.d., 161), the essay included about one hundred questions on different topics. No manuscript of the work has been found.

The work is listed in the following classical bibliographies: Ṭūsī's *al-Fihrist* (n.d., 161), Ibn Shahrāshūb's *Ma'ālim al-ʿulamā'* (1380 AH, 115), and Āqā Buzurg Ṭihrānī's *al-Dharīʿa* (1403 AH).

57. Mukhtaṣar akhbār al-Mukhtār ibn Abī ʻUbayd(a) al-Thaqafī (C)

"A brief report of Mukhtār ibn Abī ʻUbayd(a) al-Thaqafī" is a work mentioned by Ṭūsī in his own *al-Fihrist* (n.d., 161). It is known as "Akhbār al-Mukhtār" (Reports of al-Mukhtār) as well (Ibn Shahrāshūb 1380 AH, 115; Adībīmihr 1384SH, 140). This is an essay concerning the adventures of Mukhtār al-Thaqafī (d. 67 AH/687 CE). No manuscript of the essay is available. Since it is not mentioned by Najāshī (d. 450 AH/1058 CE) and is mentioned toward the end of Ṭūsī's *al-Fihrist*, it has been speculated that it was written after Najāshī's death; that is, in the last decade of Ṭūsī's life (Riḍādād and Ṭabāṭabā'ī 1387 SH, 67).

The essay is listed in the following classical bibliographies: Ṭūsī's *al-Fihrist* (n.d., 161), Ibn Shahrāshūb's *Ma'ālim al-ʻulamā'* (1380 AH, 115), and Āqā Buzurg Ṭihrānī's *al-Dharīʻa* (1403 AH, 1:348).

58. Maqtal al-Ḥusayn (C)

"The murder of Ḥusayn" is a work mentioned by Ṭūsī in his own *al-Fihrist* (n.d., 161). It is also known as "Mukhtaṣar fī maqtal al-Ḥusayn" (The brief on the murder of Ḥusayn) (Ibn Shahrāshūb 1380AH, 115) and "Maqtal Abī ʻAbd Allāh al-Ḥusayn" (The murder of Abī ʻAbd Allāh al-Ḥusayn) (Āqā Buzurg Ṭihrānī 1403 AH, 22:27). This is a historical essay about the events of Karbala during which the Imam al-Ḥusayn and his family and companions were murdered or imprisoned. Since it is not mentioned by Najāshī (d. 450 AH/1058 CE) and is mentioned toward the end of Ṭūsī's *al-Fihrist*, it has been speculated that it was written after Najāshī's death; that is, the last decade of Ṭūsī's life (Riḍādād and Ṭabāṭabā'ī 1387 SH, 67). We have not found any manuscript or copy of the work, although some people have claimed that it has been published (Adībīmihr 1384 SH, 146), but this seems to be a slip of the pen.

The work is listed in the following classical bibliographies: Ṭūsī's *al-Fihrist* (n.d., 161), Ibn Shahrāshūb's *Ma'ālim al-'ulamā'* (1380 AH, 115), and Āqā Buzurg Ṭihrānī's *al-Dharī'a* (1403 AH, 22:27).

Part Four: Bibliography of Secondary Sources

In this section, we introduce secondary sources on Ṭūsī in European languages, Arabic, and Persian.

4.1. European Languages

4.1.1. Theology

English

Books:

1. Hasan ibn Yusuf Ali ibn Mutahhar al Hilli. 1928. *Al Babul hadi ashar: a treatise on the principles of Shi'ite Theology*. Translated by William McElwee Miller. London: Royal Asiatic Society.

Papers: not found.

Dissertations and Theses: not found.

German

Books: not found.

Papers: not found.

Dissertations and Theses: not found.

French

Books: not found.

Papers: not found.

Dissertations and Theses: not found.

4.1.2. Hadith studies

English

Books: not found.

Papers: not found.

Dissertations and Theses: not found.

German

Books: not found.

Papers: not found.

Dissertations and Theses: not found.

French

Books: not found.

Papers: not found.

Dissertations and Theses: not found.

4.1.3. Quranic Sciences

English

Books: not found.

Papers:

1. Rahmani, Ahmad. 2009. "The Shiʿi Approach to the Interpretation of the Qur'an: Two Classical Commentaries." *Message of Thaqalayn Autumn*, Vol. 10. No. 3: 43-68.
2. ZabihZadeh, Ali Naghi. 2014. "Shi'a Authorities in the Age of the Minor Occultation, Part IV: Shaykh Tusi". Translated by Marzieh Ahmadi. *Message of Thaqalayn Autumn*, Vol. 15. No. 3: 59-86.
3. Bagher, Alireza and Hossein Baghalian. 2016. "Synonym from Shaykh Tusi's perspective with emphasis on tafsir al-tibyan". *Modern journal of language teaching methods*, Vol. 6: 110-118.
4. Baghalian, Hossein. 2021. "Introducing Shaykh Tusi's hermeneutic perspective in interpreting the revelation words and predicates with an emphasis on al-tibyan fi tafsir al-Quran". *International Journal of Multicultural and Multireligious Understanding*, Vol. 8, Iss. 4: 233-247.
5. Al-Hasnawi, 'Ali 'Abdel Fattah. 2021. "The effect of Sibawayh s purely opinions on the explanation on the interpretation of the Qur'an for Tusi (460) AH" *Journal of Babylon Center for Humanities Studies*, Vol. 11, Iss. 1: 715-768.

Dissertations and Theses: not found.

German

Books: not found.

Papers: not found.

Dissertations and Theses: not found.

French

Books: not found.

Papers: not found.

Dissertations and Theses: not found.

4.1.4. Principle of jurisprudence

English

Books: not found.

Papers: not found.

Dissertations and Theses: not found.

German

Books: not found.

Papers: not found.

Dissertations and Theses: not found.

French

Books: not found.

Papers: not found.

Dissertations and Theses: not found.

4.1.5. Methodology

English

Books: not found.

Papers: not found.

Dissertations and Theses

German

Books: not found.

Papers: not found.

Dissertations and Theses: not found.

French

Books: not found.

Papers: not found.

Dissertations and Theses: not found.

4.1.6. Politics

English

Books: not found.

Papers: not found.

Dissertations and Theses:

1. Al-Qazwini, Jawdat K. 1997. *The religious establishment in Ithna'ashari Shi'ism: A study in scholarly and political development.* PhD thesis. SOAS University of London.

Abstract

This thesis deals mainly with the historical development of the religious institution of Ithnaashari Shi'ism in both its scholarly and political aspects. It is divided into six chapters. The word "school" has been used to describe the place in which such an institution had flourished due to the activities of its fuqaha' in response to their turbulent history, whether it was in Iraq, in Bilad al-Sham (Greater Syria, i.e., Syria and Lebanon) or in Iran. Chapter one deals with the Baghdad School. It includes a study of the scholarly development right from the begining of the fuqaha' institution during Shaykh al-Mufid's times (d. 413/1022) and ending with Shaykh al-Tusi (d. 460/1068). Chapter two follows the development of this scholarly renaissance at the hands of the Hilla fuqaha starting with Ibn Idris al-Hilli's time (d. 598/1201) and ending with Fakhr al-Muhaqiqqin ibn al-'Allama al-Hilli (d. 771/1369) and investigates the relationship between the religious institution and the Mongol invaders of Iraq and the ideological influence of the Ithna'ashari fuqaha' on the leaders of the invaders. Chapter three, on the Jabal 'Amil school, deals in part with the unsettled period of the Mamluk state, its struggle against the Mongols, and the internal situation of the Shi'a vis-a-vis the Mamluks. It also deals in part with the influence of the Jabal 'Amil fuqaha' on the Safawid state after these fuqaha' had migrated there. Particular attention is paid to the role of Shaykh al-Karaki (d. 940/1533) and his attempt to build a religious institution inside Safawid Iran and the opposition that he met. The chapter ends with a study of the Akhbari Movement in its first stage, during the time of Muhammad Amin al-Astarabadi (d. 1033/1624).

Chapter four focuses on the Najaf School, which had started about two hundred years before as an intellectual school. The development and activities of this school from the beginning of the thirteenth/nineteenth century, are discussed, as is its position regarding the emergence of the Wahhabi Movement, the Akhbari Movement (in its second phase), and the Shaykhi Movement. The chapter also deals with the political activity of the fuqaha' in their struggle against the Qajari state, which had been manifested in the fatwa prohibiting tobacco and in the Constitutional Movement. Chapter five deals with the struggle of the Najaf fuqaha' from the start of the Republican period (1958) until the beginning of the 1990s. This is preceded by an introductory remark concerning the position taken by the fuqaha' towards the British forces who entered Iraq after the First World War and the events of the Iraqi Revolution of 1920. Chapter six has been dedicated to a study of the Qumm school. It looks at the historical development of that city, with particular attention to the role of Shaykh 'Abd al-Karim al-Ha'iri al-Yazdi (d. 1355/1936) in supervising an elite of mujtahids who have participated in the renewal of this city. (Abstract shortened by ProQuest.).

German

Books: not found.

Papers: not found.

Dissertations and Theses: not found.

French

Books: not found.

Papers: not found.

Dissertations and Theses: not found.

4.1.7. On Tusi's works

English

Books

1. Al-Tusi, Muhammad ibn al-Hasan. 1987. *Tenets of Islam*. Accra: Islamic Seminary.

2. Al-Tusi, Muhammad ibn al-Hasan. 2008. *Al-Nihayah: a concise description of Islamic law and legal opinions (al-Nihaya fi Mujarrad al-Fiqh wa al-Fatawa)*. London: ICAS Press.

3. Al-Tusi, Muhammad ibn al-Hasan, Alam al- Hoda, Aloys Sprenger, Mawlawi 'Abd al-Ḥaqq and Ġulām Qādir. 1854. *Tusy's List of Shy'ah books and 'Alam Al-Hoda's Notes on Shy'ah biography*. Calcutta.

4. Hasan ibn Yusuf Ali ibn Mutahhar al Hilli. 1928. *Al Babul hadi ashar: a treatise on the principles if Shi'ite Theology*. Translated by William McElwee Miller. London: Royal Asiatic Society.

Papers: none.

1. Ansari, Hassan, and Sabine Schmidtke. 2014. *Al-Shaykh al-Ṭūsī: His Writings on Theology and their Reception*. In Daftary, Farhad and Gurdofarid Miskinzoda, ed. 2014. *The study of Shi'i Islam: history, theology and law*. London and New York: I.B. Tauris, New York: Palgrave Macmillan.

German

Books: not found.

Papers: not found.

Dissertations and Theses: not found.

French

Books: not found.

Papers: not found.

Dissertations and Theses: not found.

4.1.8. On Tusi's life

English

Books: not found.

Papers: not found.

Dissertations and Theses

1. Ramyar, Muhammad. 1977. *Shaykh Tusi: the life and works of a Shi'ite leader*. University of Edinburgh.

Abstract

Shaykh Tusi (Abu Ja'far Muhammad) lived in the period which was marked by great activity and important changes in the whole of the Islamic world, between A.H.385/A.D.995 and 460/1067, barely longer than two-thirds of a century. He was born in Tus and lived there until he was 23 years of age, then he emigrated to Baghdad (408/1017). Certainly, when TusI arrived in Baghdad, he knew the elements and the basis of literature and theology (kalaro), as he was able to be an advanced student of al-Mufid. At that time, the Buwayhids were in power, Shiite scholars and libraries were crowded, assemblies for discussions and debates were packed. The leadership of the Ja'farites was with al-Mufld. For 28 years (1017-1044), he had busied himself in Baghdad, studying, teaching, and writing; and after the death of al-Kurtada (436/1044), he took over the presidency of Shiites in Baghdad for the next 12 years. At the time, his scholarly fame gave him such a stature that the caliph granted him the seat of kalam. During the leadership of Tusi, the Buwayhids' power fell into decline and Tusi faced an unpleasant situation. Finally, the position of the Shiites went from bad to worse, as all of his books and papers were put to the torch, and Tusi, consequently, left Baghdad and went to Najaf (448/1056). He, therefore, settled in Najaf and made that city the fixed centre for Shiite instruction. He lived in Najaf for 12 years until his death (460/1067).

German

Books: not found.

Papers: not found.

Dissertations and Theses: not found.

French

Books: not found.

Papers: not found.

❖

4.2. Arabic language

4.2.1 Theology

Books: not found.

Papers: not found.

4.2.1.1. Other studies

Books: not found.

Papers: not found.

4.2.2. Jurisprudence

Books: not found.

Papers: not found.

4.2.3. Women studies

Books: not found.

Papers

1. Kazim Zahid, ʿAbd al-Amir. 1423 AH. "Manhaj al-Shaykh al-Tusi fi Kitabi al-Khilafa fi al-fiqh" [The approach of Shaykh al-Tusi in his book al-khilafa on jurisprudence]. *Fiqh Ahl al-bayt*, no. 27: 195-248.

4.2.4. Hadith studies

Books: not found.

Papers

1. Al-Muzaffar, ʿAli ʿAbd al-Husayn and Sabah Khayri ʿArdawi. 1440 AH. "Athar al-zaman wa al-makan fi fahm-i al-nas al-hadith ʿind al-Tusi" [The effect of time and space in understanding the hadith text according to al-Tusi]. *Adab al-kufa*, no. 37: 563-584.

2. Al-Hasani, al-Shaykh Khalid Ghaguri. 1438 AH. "Qira'at al-nas al-hadithi bayn al-Hur al-ʿamili wa al-Shaykh al-Tusi" [Reading the hadith text between al-Hurr al-Amili and Shaykh al-Tusi]. *Al-Minhaj*, no, 83 & 84: 93-120.

3. Qadi ʿAskar, al-Sayyid ʿAli. 1420 AH. "Al-Shaykh al-Tusi wa-turath al-hadithi" [Shaykh al-Tusi and his hadith heritage]. *ʿUlum al-hadith*, no. 6: 120-167.

4. Al-Madadi al-Musawi, al-Sayyid Muhammad Kazim. 1439 AH. "Ru'yat hawl hami al-riwayat ʿala al-taqiyya ʿind al-Shaykh al-Tusi" [A Vision about considering narrations on the taqiyya under Shaykh al-Tusi]. Translated by Hashim Marqal. *Al-Ijtiahd wa-l-tajdid*, no. 45: 184-199.

4.2.5. History

Books: not found.

Papers: not found.

4.2.6. Quranic Sciences

Books:

1. Zaidi, Kasid Yasir. 2004. *Manhaj al-Shaykh Abi Ja'far al-Tusi fi tafsir al-Qur'an al-karim: dirasa lughawiyya nahwiyya balaghiyya* [The approach of Shaykh Abi Ja'far al-Tusi in the interpretation of Quran: a linguistic, grammatical, rhetorical study]. Baghdad: Bayt al-Hikma.
2. Khadir, Ja'far. 1378 SH. *al-Shaykh al-Tusi mufasiran* [Shaykh Al-Tusi as a Quranic exegete]. Qom: Daftar Tablighat Islami.

Papers

1. Khayyat, 'Ali. 2011-2012. "Manhaj Shaykh Tusi al-nahwi fi al-tibyan" [Shaykh Tusi's grammar approach in al-tibyan]. *Dirasat al-adabiyya*, no. 1,3,4: 110-138.
2. Khadir, Ja'far. 1369 SH. "Tafsir al-Quran bi-l-Qur'an 'ind al-Shaykh -al-Tusi" [Interpretation of the Quran by the Quran according to Shaykh al-Tusi]. *Risalat al-Quran*, no.3: 26-42.
3. Al-Khamisi, 'Abd 'Ali Husayn. 1422 AH. "Al-Abhath wa-l-dirasat: al-Shaykh al-Tusi wa-manhajuh fi al-qira'at" [Research and studies: Shaykh al-Tusi and his method in Quranic recitations]. *Al-Dhakha'ir*, no.10: 85-138.
4. Khadir, Ja'far. 1416 AH. "Tafsir al-Quran bi-l-sunna 'ind al-Shaykh al-Tusi ma' wasf mujmal li-tafsir al-tibyan" [Interpretation of the Quran by the tradition according to Shaykh al-Tusi with a

summarized description of *Tafsir al-Tibyan*]. *Qadaya Islamiyya Mu'asira*, no.2: 121-148.

5. Karidi Kundawi, Sa'd and Na'im Kazim Ihsan. 2017. "Athar qarinat al-rabt fi tawjih al-ma'ni 'ind al-Shaykh al-Tusi fi tafsir al-tibyan" [The effect of relational evidence for justification of meaning for al-Shaykh al-Tusi in al-Tibyan exegesis]. *Al-Qadisiyya fi al-adab wa-l-ma'lum al-tarbawiyya*, no. 16 (1): 9-36.

6. 'Atiyya, 'Ali Jabbar. 2005. "Kitab al-'adad: manhaj al-Shaykh al-Tusi dirasat li-rawafid mufasir 'ilmi" [Book of issue: The method of Shaykh al-Tusi, a study of the tributaries of a scientific interpreter]. *Al-Hikmat (Baghdad)*, no. 40:195.

4.2.7. On Tusi's works

Books

1. Ibn Shahrashub, Muhammad ibn 'Ali. 1383 SH. *Kitab ma'alim al-'ulama' fi fihrist kutub al-shi'a wa-asma' al-Musnifin minhum qadiman wa-hadithan (tatimma kitab al-fihrist li-Shaykh abi Ja'far al-Tusi)* [The book ma'alim al-'ulama on the list of Shiite books and the names of the authors both old and new (a supplement for Shaykh al-Tusi's list)]. Qom: al-Fiqaha.

2. Hashimi Shahrudi, Sayyid Mahmud. 1383 SH. *Al-Mu'jam al-fiqhi li-kutub al-Shaykh al-Tusi* [tra]. Qom: Mu'assisa Da'irat al-Ma'arif al-Fiqh al-Islami.

3. Tabarsi, Fadl ibn Hasan. 1390 SH. *Al-Mu'talif min al-mukhtalaf bayn a'immat al-salaf wa-huwa muntakhab al-khilaf li-l-Shaykh al-Tusi* [A selection of *al-Khilaf* by al-Shaykh al-Tusi]. Mashhad: Bunyad Pazhuhish-hayi Islami Astan Quds Razavi.

Papers

1. Malikian, Muhammad Baqir. 1438 AH. "Al-Shaykh al-Tusi wa-takmil kitab al-fihrist" [Shaykh al-Tusi and the supplement of the book *al-Fihrist*]. *Al-Ijtihad wa-l-tajdid*, no. 43: 97-102.

2. ʿAbd al-Amir, Kazim Zahid. 1423 AH. "Manhaj al-Shaykh al-Tusi fi kitab al-khilafa fi al-fiqh" [Shaykh al-Tusi's approach of in his book *al-Khilaf fi l-fiqh*]. *Fiqh ahl al-bayt*, no. 27: 195-248.

3. Lawasani, Ahmad. 1963. "Fi maktabatina" [In our school]. *Dirasat adabiyya*, no. 2: 197-210.

4. Shubayri Zanjani, Sayyid Muhammad Jawad. 1420 AH. "Masadir al-Shaykh al-Tusi fi kitab tahdhib al-ahkam" [Al-Shaykh al-Tusi's sources of in the book *Tahdhib al-ahkam*]. *ʿUlum al-hadith*, no. 6: 168-224.

4.2.8. On Tusi's life

Books

1. Hasan ʿIsa, Hakim. 1975. *Al-Shaykh al-Ṭusi Abu Jaʿfar Muḥammad ibn al-Ḥasan,* 385-460 *AH*. Najaf.

Papers

1. Tihrani, Aqa buzurg. 1342 SH. "Shaykh Tusi". Translated by Sayyid ʿAli Akbar Waʿiz Musawi. *Nama Astan Quds*, no. 14: 16-26.

2. Al-Shakiri, Husayn. 1422 AH. "Min aʿlam madrasa ahl al-bayt: Shaykh al-ta'ifat al-Tusi" [Among the notables of Ahl al-Bayt School: Shaykh al-Tusi]. *Risalat al-thaqalayn*, no. 38: 192-205.

3. Shubayyri Zanjani, Sayyid Muhammad Jawad. 1436 AH. "Al-Ta'thir wa-l-ta'aththur bayn al-shaykh al-Mufid wa-l-Sayyid al-Murtada w-l-shaykh al-Tusi" [The mutual influence of al-Shaykh al-Mufid, al-

Sayyid al-Murtada, and al-Shaykh al-Tusi]. *Al-ʿAqida,* no. 3: 412-416.

4. Al-Asʿad, Bin ʿAli. 1421 AH. "Al-Shaykh al-Tusi mujadadan" [al-Shaykh al-Tusi again]. *Al-Minhaj,* no. 20: 74-103.

5. Ridazada ʿAskari, Zahra. 1431 AH. "Dawr al-Shaykh al-Tusi fi l-nihdat al-ʿilmiyya al-tatawwur al-fiqh unmuzaj" [Al-Shaykh al-Tusi's role in the scientific movement, the development of jurisprudence as a model]. *Al-Ijtihad wa-l-tajdid,* no. 11-12: 408-425.

6. Fadlullah, ʿAli Muhammad Jawad. 1425 AH. "Tarikh: mahatat fi hayat al-Shaykh al-Tusi al-ʿilmiyya" [History: Stations in Shaykh al-Tusi's scientific life]. *Baqiyyat allah,* no. 151: 73-75.

7. Al-ʿAmidi al-Husayni, al-Sayyid Thamir Hashim. 1418 AH. "Dawr al-Shaykh al-Tusi fi ʿulum al-shariʿat al-islamiyya 1" [The role of Shaykh al-Tusi in the sciences of Islamic law 1]. *Turathuna,* no. 4: 36-65.

8. Al-ʿAmidi al-Husayni, al- Thamir Hashim. 1419 AH. "Dawr al-Shaykh al-Tusi fi ʿulum al-shariʿat al-islamiyya 2" [The role of Shaykh al-Tusi in the sciences of Islamic law 2]. *Turathuna,* no. 1-2: 241-284.

9. Al-ʿAmidi al-Husayni, al-Sayyid Thamir Hashim. 1419 AH. "Dawr al-Shaykh al-Tusi fi ʿulum al-shariʿat al-islamiyya 3" [The role of Shaykh al-Tusi in the sciences of Islamic law 3]. *Turathuna,* no. 3-4: 105-155.

10. Al-ʿAmidi al-Husayni, al-Sayyid Thamir Hashim. 1420 AH. "Dawr al-Shaykh al-Tusi fi ʿulum al-shariʿat al-islamiyya 4" [The role of Shaykh al-Tusi in the sciences of Islamic law 4]. *Turathuna,* no. 1: 94-120.

11. Al-ʿAmidi al-Husayni, al-Sayyid Thamir Hashim. 1420 AH. "Dawr al-Shaykh al-Tusi fi ʿulum al-shariʿat al-islamiyya 5" [The role of

Shaykh al-Tusi in the sciences of Islamic law 5]. *Turathuna,* no. 3-4: 102-123.

12. Al-ʿAmidi al-Husayni, al-Sayyid Thamir Hashim. 1420 AH. "Dawr al-Shaykh al-Tusi fi ʿulum al-shariʿat al-islamiyya 6" [The role of Shaykh al-Tusi in the sciences of Islamic law 6]. *Turathuna,* no. 3-4: 153-171.

13. Nasser, A.L.A.J. 2018. "Muhammad ibn al-Hasan al-Tusi, nash'atihi wa-atharih al-ʿilmiyya" [Tusi: his origins and his scientific implication]". *The Arab Gulf,* no. 46: 3-4.

14. Muhammad al-Khadiri, Mahmud. 1374 AH. "Al-Shaykh al-Tusi". *Risalat al-islam,* no. 1: 40-46.

15. Al-Qays, Qays. 1423 AH. "Al-Shaykh al-Tusi". *Afaq al-hadaraht al-islamiyya,* no. 10: 323-380.

4.2.9. Literature and poetry

Books: not found.

Papers

1 Hanawi Saʿdun, Nadiyya. 2007. "Malamih riwayat al-shiʿr fi al-Shaykh al-Tusi's Amali" [Features of narrating poetry in Tusi's book Amali]. *Adab al-mustansariyya,* no. 47: 684-709.

2. Khayyat, ʿAli. 1431-1432 AH. "Madhhab al-Shaykh al-Tusi al-nahwi" [Tusi's syntactic approach]. *Al-Lughat al-ʿarabiyya wa-adabuha,* no. 11: 49-70.

❖

4.3. Persian language

4.3.1. Theology

Books: not found.

Papers: not found.

4.3.1.1. Prophecy

Books

1. Rahimuf, Afdal al-Din. 1396 SH. *'Ismat anbia az nazar Shaykh Tusi wa-Fakhr Razi* [The infallibility of the prophets according to Shaykh Tusi and Fakhr Razi]. Qom: Nashr al-Mustafa.

4.3.1.2. Imamate

Books

1. Murtadawi Chupanan, Ghulam Rida. 1398 SH. *Jaygah ahlbayt dar tafsir tibyan Shaykh Tusi* [The position of Ahl al-Bayt in Shaykh Tusi's tafsir tibyan (Al-Tibbyan fi tafsir al-Qur'an)]. Tehran: Rah Dukturi, Sanjish wa-Danish.

Papers

1. Manzur al-Ajdad, Sayyid Muhammad Husayn. 1380-81 SH. "Shurish Basasiri wa-payamadhayi an barayi Shi'ayan Baghdad" [The Basasiri Riot and its consequences for Shiites of Baghdad]. *Zaban wa-adabiyyat Farsi*, no. 35-39: 87-110.
2. Mustafawi, Asadullah and Akbar Rusta'i. 1399 AH. "Rawish-shinasi kalami Shaykh Tusi dar pasukh bi shubahat mahdawiyyat ba ta'kid bar kitab al-Ghayba" [Shaykh Tusi's theological methodology in

response to suspicions about Mahdism with a focus on the book *al-Ghayba*]. *Intizar maw'ud*, no. 68: 55-82.

3. Sidaqat Kashfi, Sayyid Muhammad Jawad and 'Abbas Humami. 1396 SH. "Muqayisa ruykard mahdawiyyat nigari Shaykh Saduq wa-Shaykh Tusi" [The comparison of the Mahdist approach of Shaykh Ṣaduq and Shaykh Tusi]. *Pazhuhish-nama Qur'an wa-hadith*, no. 20: 25-48.
4. Yusifiyan, Hasan and Muhammad Sadiq 'Alipur. 1390 SH. "Barrisi-yi tatbiqi falsafi-yi imamat az manzar Shaykh Mufid, Sayyid Murtada wa-Shaykh Tusi" [A comparative study of the philosophy of Imamate according to Shaykh Mufid, Sayyid Murtada and Shaykh Tusi]. *Andisha-yi nuwin dini*, no. 24: 37-64.
5. Wilayati, Maryam and Shadi Nafisi. 1393 SH. "Ruykard Shaykh Tusi nisbat bi pishiniyan dar mas'ala-yi riwayat ta'wili dar haqq Ahlibayt (a)" [Shaykh Tusi's approach to his predecessors on the issue of hadiths about esoteric exegeses of the Quran concerning Ahl Al-Bayt]. *Amuza-hayi Qur'ani*, no. 20: 103-128.

4.3.1.3. God and His attributes

Books

1. Bayt Sayah, Zaynab. 1399 SH. *Rawish-hayi istidlal Quran karim dar ithbat sani' ba tikya bar dīdgāh-hayi 'Allama Tabataba'i wa-Shaykh Tusi* [Argumentative methods of the holy Quran in proving the creator relying on the perspectives of 'Allāma Tabataba'i and Shaykh Tusi]. Tehran: Danishyaran Iran.

Papers

1. Za'firani Zadi, Sa'id and Ghulam Husayn A'rabi. 1396 SH. "Barrisi-yi tatbiqi-yi ru'yat khuda dar tafsir Shaykh Tusi wa-tafsir Maturidi" [A comparative study of the vision of God in the commentary of

Shaykh Tusi and the commentary of Maturidi]. *Pazhuhish-hayi tafsir tatbiqi*, no. 6: 51-69.

2. Parsa, ʿAlirida, Ghulam Husayn Khidiri, Nasir Muhammadi and Khalil Mullajawadi. 1399 SH. "Barrisi-yi tatbiqi-yi didgah Shaykh Tusi wa-Ghazali dar mawrid jaygah ʿaql dar maʿrifat bi khuda dar gustara-yi intizar bashar az din" [A comparative study of the perspectives of Shaykh Tusi and Ghazali on the place of reason in knowledge of God in the scope of man's expectation of religion]. *Andisha-yi nuwin dini*, no. 61: 65-86.

4.3.1.4. Jurisprudence

Books: not found.

Papers: not found.

4.3.1.5. Women Fasting (Ṣawm)

Books: not found.

Papers

1. Sharifpur, Najmi and Bimanʿali Dihghan Mangabadi. 1394 SH. "Barrisi-yi tatbiqi hukm nikah mutʿa az didgah Shaykh Tusi wa-Abu Hanifa" [A comparative study of the ruling on temporary marriage from the perspective of Shaykh Tusi and Abu Ḥanifa]. *Mabani-yi fiqhi-yi huquq islami*, no. 15: 31-55.
2. Dihqan, Majid and Hasanʿali ʿAli Akbariyan. 1397 SH. "Tahlil tarikhi-yi naqsh Shaykh Tusi dar ʿurfi shudan nafaqi-yi zawja" [Historical analysis of Shaykh Tusi's role in secularization of the wife's alimony]. *Fiqh muqarin*, no. 11: 5-28.

3. Tavalla'i, 'Ali. 1389 SH. "Qadi shudan zan dar fiqh Shaykh Tusi: risha-yabi wa-tahlil" [Women's judgment in Shaykh Tusi's jurisprudence, rooting, and analysis]. *Fiqh wa-usul*, no. 85: 29-48.

4.3.1.6. Methodology

Books: none.

1. Khushdil, 'Alirida. 1398 SH. *Sirr ahkam dini* [The secret of religious rules]. Tehran: Arun.

Papers

1. Madadi Musawi, Sayyid Muhammad Kazim. 1396 SH. "Barrisi-yi sayr tarikhi-yi shiklgiri-yi furu' jadid dar fiqh mutaqaddim Shi'a; barrisi-yi tahawwulat tamkin" [A study of the historical course of the formation of new branches in the early Shiite jurisprudence; a study of the developments of the issue of obedience]. *Fiqh*, no. 4: 83-100.

2. Madadi Musawi, Sayyid Muhammad Kazim. 1393 SH. "Sayr tahawwul haml bar taqiyya dar fiqh az dawra-yi Shaykh Tusi ta dawra-yi Muqaddas Ardibili: tahawwul az tariqiyyat bi mawdu'iyyat" [The evolution of considering as taqiyya in jurisprudence from the period of Shaykh Tusi to the period of Muqaddas Ardabili: a transformation from tariqiyyat to mawdu'iyyat]. *Fiqh*, no. 4: 95-109.

3. Madadi Musawi, Sayyid Muhammad Kazim. 1393 SH. "Fardiyya-iy darbara-yi hama-yi riwayat bar taqiyya az manzar Shaykh Tusi" [A hypothesis about considering hadiths as taqiyya from the perspective of Shaykh Tusi]. *Fiqh*, no. 3: 93-111.

4. Turkashwand, Sajjad and Muhammad Kakawand. 1399 SH. "Mabani-yi fiqhi-yi rujhan masalih 'umumi bar masalih fardi ba muraji'a bi ara' Imam Khomeini wa-Shaykh Tusi" [Jurisprudential

principles of preferring public interests over individual interests by referring to the opinions of Imam Khomeini and Shaykh Tusi]. *Hukumat islami*, no. 96: 77-100.

4.3.1.7. Other studies

Books

1. Yazdi Mutlaq Fadil, Mahmud, ed. 1399 SH. *Andisha-hayi kalami-yi Shaykh Tusi* [Shaykh Tusi's theological thoughts]. Mashhad: Razavi University of Islamic Sciences.
2. Labbaf, ʻAli. 1392 SH. *Barrisi-yi sanad ziyarat ʻAshura dar mirath maktub Shaykh Tusi* [A study of the chain of transmission of ziyarat ʻAshura in the written heritage of Shaykh Tusi]. Tehran: Munir.
3. Raja'ifard, Abulfadl. 1399 SH. Mirath maktub Shiʻa dar panj qarn nukhust: tabyin sayr shiklgiri wa-tahawwul athar shiʻayan dar hawza-hayi hadith mukhtalif bar asas du fihrist Najashi wa-Shaykh Tusi [Shiite written heritage in the first five centuries: explaining the course of formation and evolution of Shiite works in the fields of different hadiths based on Najashi's and Shaykh Tusi's al-Fihrist]. Tehran: Nigaristan Andyshih.
4. Pakatchi, Ahmad. 1385 SH. *Makatib fiqh imami-yi Iran pas az Shaykh Tusi ta pagiri-yi maktab Hilli* [Schools of Iranian Imami jurisprudence after Shaykh Tusi until the Hilla school was established]. Tehran: Imam Sadiq University.
5. Dilbari, ʻAli. 1390 SH. *Mabani-yi rafʻ taʻarud akhbar az didgah Shaykh Tusi dar Istibsar* [Grounds of removing contradictions between hadiths in Shaykh Tusi's view] [tra]. Mashhad: Razavi University of Islamic Sciences.
6. Shaykh Tusi, Muhammad ibn Hasan. 1393 SH. *Fiqh tatbiqi: tarjuma-yi bab wasaya az kitab al-Khilaf Shaykh Tusi* [Comparative

jurisprudence: translation and explanation of the chapter of inheritance and will of the book *al-Khilaf* by Shaykh Tusi]. Translated by Muhammad Mahdi Qasimi Sutih. Qom: Awayi Zistan.

7. Shaykh Tusi, Muhammad ibn Hasan. 1396 SH. *Fiqh tatbiqi-yi irth wa-wasiyyat: tarjuma wa-sharh az kitab al-Khilaf Shaykh Tusi* [Comparative jurisprudence of inheritance, will: explanation, translation of problem solving from the book *al-Khilaf* by Shaykh Tusi]. Translated by Akbar Nayibzadi. Tehran: Khursandi.

8. Qa'imi Khiraq, Muhsin and Muhammad Lurinizhad. 1395 SH. *Andisha-hayi tatbiqi-yi irth wa-wasiyyat: tarjuma wa-tahqiq bab al-fara'id wa-al-wasaya kitab al-Khilaf Shaykh Tusi* [Comparative thoughts of inheritance and will: translation and research of the chapters *al-Fara'iḍ* and *al-Waṣaya* of the book al-Khilaf by Shaykh Tusi]. Tehran: Khursandi.

9. ʿArabniya, Muhammad Sadiq. 1373 SH. *Barrisi-yi masa'il hudud az kitab al-Khilaf marhum Shaykh Tusi* [Examining the issues of hudud from the book al-Khilaf by Shaykh Tusi]. Tehran: Sazman Tabliqat Islami.

10. Mustaqimiyan, Abulfadl. 1380 SH. *Jahad az didgah Shaykh Tusi* [Jihad from the perspective of Shaykh Tusi]. Gorgan: Makhtumquli Faraghi.

11. Sharifi Nasir, Dariyush. 1385 SH. *Talaq khulʿ: nahwa-yi raha'i-yi zan az badkhulqi-yi shawhar (tarjuma wa-sharh kitab al-khulʿ az al-Mabsut Shaykh Tusi)* [The divorce of khulʿ: how to free a woman from her husband's bad temper and translation and explanation of the book of al-khulʿ of al-Mabsut by Shaykh Tusi]. Qom: Shakir.

Papers

1. Amirkhani, ʿAli. 1393 SH. "Tatawwur maʿrifat idtirari dar madrisa-yi kalami imamiyyi dar Baghdad (az Nubakhtiyan ta Shaykh Tusi)"

[The evolution of necessary knowledge in Imami theological school (from Nubakhtiyan to Shaykh Tusi)]. *Tahqiqat kalami*, no. 4: 23-40.

2. Turan, Imdad. 1393 SH. "Hayat pishin insan az didgah mutakalliman Baghdad" [The previous life of man from the perspective of Baghdad's theologians]. *Tahqiqat kalami*, no. 6: 7-26.

3. Muhammad Ja'fari, Rasul. 1396 SH. "Mutali'a-yi tatbiqi-yi didgah Shaykh Saduq wa-Shaykh Mufid wa-didgah Sayyid Murtada wa-Shaykh Tusi darbara-yi bada'" [A comparative study of the perspectives of Shaykh Saduq and Shaykh Mufid and the perspectives of Sayyid Murtada and Shaykh Tusi about Bada']. *Shi'a-pazhuhi*, no. 12: 23-48.

4. Tawakkuli Muhammadi, Murtada and Hamid Riza Shari'atmadari. 1393 SH. "'Aqlgirayi wa-nassgirayi dar kalam islami ba barrisi-yi didgah Shaykh Tusi wa-Ibn Idris" [Rationalism and textualism in Islamic theology by examining the perspectives of Shaykh Tusi and Ibn Idris]. *Pazhuhish-nama-yi kalami*, no. 1: 27-48.

5. Karimi, 'Alirida and Manuchihr Samadiwand. 1393 SH. "Barrisi-yi 'awamil faraz wa-furud fiqh Shi'a pas az Shaykh Tusi wa-mutali'a-yi sharayit ta'thirguzar bar rushd dubara-yi an" [Examining the causes of the rise and fall of Shiite jurisprudence after Shaykh Tusi and studying the conditions affecting its regrowth]. *Tarikhnama-yi Iran ba'd az Islam*, no. 9: 183-203.

4.3.2. Hadith

Books

1. Hidayati, Amir Rida. 1399 SH. *Ta'wid sanad dar turuq Shaykh Tusi wa-shaykh Saduq wa-Najashi* [Exchange of the chain of transmission on the ways of Shaykh Tusi and Shaykh Ṣaduq and Najashi, may God have mercy on them]. Qom: Ayat.

2. Bahrayni, Sayyid Mujtaba. 1390 SH. *Hadith sada-yi panjum: Skaykh Tusi* [Fifth-century hadith: Shaykh Tusi (may God exalt his position)]. Mashhad: Yusuf Fatima.

Papers

1. Huda'i, 'Alirida. 1375 SH. "Ibn Idris Hilli wa-kitab al-Sara'ir" [Ibn Idris Hilli and the book *al-Sara'ir*]. *Maqalat wa-barrisiha*, no. 59-60: 119-128.
2. Qurbani Muqaddam, Muhammad. 1395 SH. "Barrisi-yi sanadi-yi ziyarat 'Ashura" [Examining the chain of transmission of ziyarat 'Ashura]. *Hadith pazhuhi*, no. 15: 77-100.
3. Shirzad, Muhammad Husayn, Muhammad Hasan Shirzad and Muhsin Musawi. 1394 SH. "Bazsazi ingara-yi asl dar nazargah Shaykh Tusi" [Reconstructing the tenet of "principle" in Shaykh Tusi's point of view]. *Pazhuhish-hayi Qur'an wa-hadith*, no. 2: 247-268.
4. Afshari, Najma and Fathiyya Fatahizada. 1391 SH. "Jaygah naqd hadith dar Wasa'il al-Shi'a" [The place of hadith criticism in *Wasa'il Al-Shi'a*]. *Tahqiqat 'ulum Qur'an wa-hadis*, no. 17: 109-144.
5. Sultanifar, Jawad et al. 1399 SH. "Tahlil ma'nayi-yi asnad 'anh wa-imkansanji-yi dilalat an bar i'tibar rawi" [Semantic analysis of "asand 'anh" and feasibility study of its implication for the credibility of the narrator]. *Mutali'at Qur'an wa-hadith*, no. 26: 129-166.
6. Izadi, 'Aliakbar, 'Aliakbar Rabi' Nataj and Mujtaba Husaynnizhad. 1395 SH. "Naqd ingara-yi taz'if Muhammad ibn 'Isa ibn 'Abid ibn Yaqtin" [The criticism of the view of unreliability of Muḥammad ibn 'Isa ibn 'Ubaid ibn Yaqtin]. *Tahqiqat 'ulum Qur'an wa-hadith*, no. 30: 1-31.

7. Hasanzada Dilgusha, Saʿid, Yaʿqub Purjamal and Muhammad Muharrami. 1399 SH. "Hamahangi haml bar taqiyya ba murajjihat akhbar ʿilajiyya dar rawiyya Shaykh al-Taʾifa" [tra]. *Pazhuhishhayi fiqhi*, no. 41: 291-308.

8. Mahdawi Yigana, Muhammad Rida, Muhammad Kazim Rahman Sitayish and Muhammad Taqi Diyari Bidguli. 1398 SH. "Tahlil mafhum wazha-yi thiqa nazd muhaddithan wa-rijaliyan mutaqaddim Shiʿa wa-jaygah madhhab dar an" [Analysis of the meaning of the word thiqa among the early Shiite transmitters of hadiths and scholars of *rijāl* and the place of religion in it]. *ʿUlum hadith*, no. 93: 51-81.

9. Muʾaddab, Rida and Kazim Zamani Pahmadani. 1396 SH. "Tahlil riwayat tafsiri muntaqili-yi ibn Fahham dar khusus kasti az aya-yi 33 Al ʿImran dar Amali Shaykh Tusi" [Analysis of the interpretive hadith transmitted by Ibn Faham regarding the shortcomings of verse 33 of Al-Imran in the Shaykh Tusi's *al-Amali*]. *Hadith-pazhuhi*, no.17: 147-164.

10. Bayat Mukhtari, Mahdi. 1390 SH. "Tadarub araʾ Shaykh Tusi wa-Najashi darbara-yi Hariz ibn ʿAbdullah Sajistani" [Conflict between the views of Shaykh Tusi and Najashi about Hariz Ibn ʿAbdullah Sajistani]. *ʿUlum Qurʾan wa-hadith*, no. 87: 65-82.

11. Rikabiyan, Rashid, Rida Ramadani and Ibrahim Salihi Hajiabadi. 1399 SH. "Iʿtibarsanji-yi tarikhi rijal Shaykh Tusi dar dabt ashab Imam Husayn" [Historical validation of Shaykh Tusi's *Rijal* in the recording of Imam Husayn's companions]. *Tarikh islam*, no. 83: 139-166.

12. Nilsaz, Nusrat and Abulfazl Rajaʾifard. 1396 SH. "Karkard fihrist-hayi Shaykh Tusi wa-Najashi dar takmil rawish Sezgin dar bazyabi-yi manabiʿ athar kuhan riwaʾi (mutaliʿa-yi mawridi: kitab al-Zuhd Husayn ibn Saʿid Ahwazi)" [The function of Shaykh Tusi's and Najashi's *Fihrist* in completing the Sezgin's method in retrieving

the sources of ancient narrative works (case study: the book of al-Zuhd Husayn ibn Sa'id Ahwazi)]. *Mutali'at fahm hadith*, no. 7: 130-156.

13. Sarshar, Muzhgan. 1392 SH. "Riwayat Bakr ibn Muhammad wa-mas'ala-yi ta'arud dar bab sizdahum rijal Shaykh Tusi" [The narrations of Bakr ibn Muhammad and the issue of conflict in the thirteenth chapter of Shaykh Tusi's *Rijal*]. *Hadith-pazhuhi*, no. 9: 153-178.
14. Adham, Radiya and Asghar Qa'idan. 1392 SH. "Jaygah rawiyan dar rijal Shaykh Tusi" [The place of hadith transmitters in Shaykh Tusi's *Rijal*]. *Tarikh farhang wa-tamaddun Islami*, no. 11: 71-90.
15. Shahpasand, Ilaha. 1395 SH. "Naqsh asma' mutashabih dar ta'arud didgah Najashi wa-Shaykh Tusi piramun Salim ibn Mukarram" [The role of similar names in the conflict of the perspectives of Najashi and Shaykh Tusi on Salim ibn Mukarram]. *Tahqiqat 'ulum Qur'an wa-hadith*, no. 29: 161-182.
16. Jalali, Mahdi and Rahima Shamshiri. 1388 SH. "Mazaya-yi fihrist Najashi bar fihrist wa-rijal Shaykh Tusi wa-barrisi-yi nisbat wa-ikhtilaf anha ba yikdigar" [The advantages of Najashi's *al-Fihrist* over Shaykh Tusi's *al-Fihrist* and *Rijal* and examining their relationship and differences with each other]. *'Ulum Qur'an wa-hadith*, no. 83: 101-120.
17. Nilsaz, Nusrat and Abulfadl Raja'ifard. 1397 SH. "Tarikhnigari maktab hadithi-yi Kufa dar panj Qarn nukhust wa-ta'thirgudhari an bar tarikhnigari islami bar asas du fihrist Najashi wa-Shaykh Tusi" [Historiography of the Kufa hadith school in the first five centuries and its influence on Islamic historiography based on Shaykh Tusi's and Najashi's *al-Fihrist*]. *Shi'a-shinasi*, no. 61: 81-118.
18. Surkha'i, Ihsan. 1394 SH. "Karburd hadith wa-riwayat dar fihrist wa-rijal pishiniyan" [The use of hadith and narration in book

catalogues and rijāl of the predecessors]. *'Ulum hadith*, no. 76: 93-119.

19. Ma'rifat, Muhammad and Muhammad Ghafurinizhad. 1396 SH. "Tahlil masdar shinasi-yi ahadith al-Ghayba Shaykh Tusi" [An analysis of the study of the sources of hadiths in Shaykh Tusi's *al-Ghayba*] [tra]. *Intizar-i Mu'ud*, no. 57: 5-28.

20. Jalali, Mahdi and Rahima Shamshiri. 1387 SH. "Barrisi-yi wa-arzyabi-yi rawish Shaykh Tusi dar naqd rijal wa-atharash" [Investigating and evaluating Shaykh Tusi's method in criticizing Rijal and his works]. *Mutali'at Islami*, no. 80: 109-142.

21. Ma'arif, Majid. 1376 SH. "Muqayisa-yi dīdgāh-hayi rijali-yi Najashi wa-Shaykh Tusi" [Comparing the rijali perspectives of Shaykh Tusi and Najashi]. *Maqalat wa-barrisiha*, no. 62: 39-58.

22. Rubati, Samana and Mahdi Jalali. 1395 SH. "Barrisi-yi tatbiqi-yi rawish Ibn Ghada'iri, Shaykh Tusi wa-Najashi dar ta'amul bar rawiyan ghayr imami" [A comparative study of the methods of Ibn Ghada'iri, Shaykh Tusi and Najashi in interaction with non-Imami transmitters of hadiths]. *'Ulum hadith*, no. 79: 144-167.

23. 'Azimzada, Tahira. 1391 SH. "Yadkard az Husayn ibn Ruh Nubakhti dar manabi' kuhan (sada-hayi 4 ta 8 hijri)" [Mentioning Husayn ibn Ruh Nubakhti in ancient sources (4th to 8th centuries AH)]. *Tarikh wa-farhang*, no. 89: 99-126.

24. Kamyabi, Muhammad Mahdi. 1393 SH. "Kawushi dar gustara-yi naql nukhustin maktubat hadithi imamyya" [An exploration of the scope of the transmission of the first Imami hadith writings]. *'Ulum hadith*, no. 72: 32-55.

4.3.3. Quranic sciences

Books

1. Muhaqiq, Muhammad Baqir. 1389 SH. *Nimuna-yi bayyinat dar sha'n nuzul ayat az nazar Shykh Tusi wa-sayir mufassirin 'amma wa-khassa* [Example of evidence about the occasions of revelation of Quranic verses in the view of Shaykh Tusi and other Sunni and Shiite exegetes] [tra]. Tehran: Islami.
2. Kumpani Zari', Mahdi. 1390 SH. *Shaykh Tusi wa-tafsir Tibyan* [Shaykh Tusi and Tafsir al-tibyan]. Tehran: Khana-yi Kitab.
3. Sultani, Muhammad. 1395 SH. *Tahlil wa-barrisi-yi mabani-yi kalami tafsir Qur'an karim bar mihwar athar Shaykh Tusi* [Analysis and study of the theological principles of the interpretation of the Holy Quran on the works of Shaykh Tusi]. Qom: Hawzeh and University Research Institute.
4. Murtadawi Chupanan, Ghulam Rida. 1398 SH. *Jaygah Ahlbayt dar tafsir Tibyan Shaykh Tusi* [The position of Ahl al-Bayt in Shaykh Tusi's Tafsiri al-tibyan (al-Tibbyan fi tafsir al-Qur'an)]. Tehran: Rah Dukturi, Sanjish wa-Danish.

Papers

1. Muhammadi Khurramabadi, Ghulam Muhammad. "Shia wa-ara'i tafsiri-yi Mu'tazila" [Shiites and Mu'tazilite exegetical opinions]. *Mutali'at Islami*, no. 68: 117-134.
2. Kariminiya, Murtada. 1390 SH. "Ma'kala-yi salana-yi yahud: barrisiyi riwayati tafsiri dar manabi' kuhan Shi'a wa-Sunni" [The Jewish annual food: a study of exegetical hadiths in old Shiite and Sunni sources] [tra]. *Pazhuhishhayi Qur'an wa-hadith*, no. 2: 119-140.
3. Mas'udiniya, Sumayya and Muhsin Qasimpur Rawandi. 1396 SH. "Ara' Mu'tazila dar mutali'a-yi tatbiqi bayn girayish tafsiri Tusi wa-

Tabarsi" [Mu'tazilite opinions in a comparative study between the exegetical tendencies of Tusi and Tabarsi]. *Pazhuhishnama-yi tafsir wa-zaban Qur'an*, no. 10: 11-34.

4. Farjami, A'zam, Zuhra Narimani and Runak Imami. 1398 SH. "Masdaryabi riwayat tafsir al-Tibyan ba tatbiq bar manabi' Shi'a wa-Sunni" [Finding the sources of the hadiths of Tafsir al-Tibyan by applying them to Shiite and Sunni sources]. *Pazhuhish-hayi Qur'an wa-hadith*, no. 1: 9-28.

5. Hajiakbari, Fatima and Muhsin Qasimpur. 1394 SH. "Barrisi-yi tatbiqi-yi mabani tafsiri Shaykh Tusi wa-Fakhr Razi wa-ta'thir an dar mawdu' naskh" [A comparative study of exegetical principles of Shaykh Tusi and Fakhr Razi]. *Pazhuhishnama-yi tafsir wa-zaban Qur'an*, no. 6: 7-22.

6. Qasimpur, Muhsin. 1388 SH. "Shaykh Tusi wa-ara' tafsiri-yi Mu'tazila" [Shaykh Tusi and Mu'tazilite exegetical views]. *Tahqiqat 'ulum Qur'an wa-hadith*, no. 11: 85-104.

7. Khalili Ashtiyani, Sumayya and 'Abas Humami. 1395 SH. "Nahwa-yi istifada Shaykh Tusi az riwayat dar tafsir al-Tibyan" [How Shaykh Tusi used hadiths in tafsir al-Tibyan]. *Pazhuhishhayi Qur'an wa-hadith*, no. 19: 1-21.

8. Najafi Liwari, Maryam and Muhsin Qasimpur. 1397 SH. "Shakhisa-hayi ruykard tafsir 'aqli Shaykh Tusi ba ta'kid bar ayat 83-149 sura-yi an'am" [Characteristics of Shaykh Tusi's rational exegetical approach with a focus on verses 83 and 149 of Sura An'am]. *Mutali'at tafsiri*, no. 34: 43-60.

9. Farid, Zahra and Amir Mahmud Anwar. 1392 SH. "Ruykard lughawi Shaykh Tusi dar tafsir Tibyan" [Shaykh Tusi's lexical approach in tafsir al-Tibyan]. *Lisan mubin*, no. 11: 18-36.

10. Rida'i Haftadar, Ghulam 'Abbas, Ibrahim Dibaji and Hasan Kazimi Sahliwani. 1396 SH. "Barrisi-yi ma'nashinasi wazha-yi salam dar

tafsir Tibyan Shaykh Tusi" [A study of the semantics of the word salam in Shaykh Tusi's tafsir al-Tibyan]. *Adab 'Arabi*, no.1: 249-260.

11. Qasimpur, Muhsin and Zaynab Radawikiya. 1398 SH. "Khastgah tarikhi-yi 'aqlgirayi az manzar Shaykh Tusi dar Tibyan wa-ta'thir an dar arzyabi riwayat tafsiri" [The historical origin of rationalism according to Shaykh Tusi in al-Tibyan and its impact on the evaluation of exegetical hadiths]. *Pazhuhish dini*, no. 39: 95-112

12. Talib Tash, 'Abd al-Majid and Layla Asadi. 1397 SH. "Ta'thirpaziri-yi Majma' al-bayan dar mabahith kalami az mufassiran wa-muhaddithan pishin ba ta'kid bar al-Tibyan Shaykh Tusi" [Influence of Majma' al-bayan in theological discussions of previous commentators and narrators with a focus on Shaykh Tusi's al-Tibyan]. *Mutali'at tarikhi Quran wa-hadith*, no. 63: 199-219.

13. 'Abbasi, Firaydun, Mustafa Ahmadifar and Muhammad Imami. 1398 SH. "Rahyafti naw bar hujjiyyat khabar wahid dar tafsir (ba ta'kid bar didgah Shaykh Tusi)" [A new approach to the authority of single-narrator hadiths in Quranic exegesis (with a focus on the view of Shaykh Tusi)]. *Amuza-hayi Qur'ani*, no. 29: 251-276.

14. 'Amari Allahyari, Zahra and Shadi Nafisi. 1393 SH. "Mabani-yi ruykard adabi dar tafsir Sayyid Murtada wa-Shaykh Tusi ba ta'kid bar al-Amali wa al-Tibyan" [Principles of literary approach in the exegesis of Sayyid Murtada and Shaykh Tusi based on al-Amali and al-Tibyan]. *Pazhuhishhayi Adabi Qur'ani*, no. 3: 103-137.

15. Kariminiya, Murtada. 1385 SH. "Shaykh Tusi wa-manabi' tafsiri-yi way dar al-Tibyan" [Shaykh Tusi and his exegetical Sources in al-Tibyan]. *Mutali'at Islami*, no. 74: 81-111.

16. Kazimi Sahliwani, Hasan, Ghulam 'Abbas Rida'i Haftadari and Ibrahim Dibaji. 1393 SH. "Ma'nashinasi Qur'an dar tafsir Tibyan

Shaykh Tusi" [The semantics of the Qur'an in Shaykh Tusi's tafsir al-Tibyan]. *'Uyun*, no. 1:25-38.

17. Baqir, 'Alirida and Fatima 'Amiri. 1397 SH. "Naqsh 'ulum balaghi dar tafsir Qur'an (mutali'a-yi mawridi-yi kinaya wa-ta'rid dar tafsir Tibyan Shaykh Tusi wa-Kashshaf Zamakhshari" [The role of rhetorical sciences in the exegesis of the Qur'an (a case study of irony and sarcasm in Shaykh Tusi's tafsir al-Tibyan and Zamakhshari's Kashshaf)]. *Pazhuhish-hayi tafsir tatbiqi*, no. 8: 39-63.
18. Qurbani Zarrin, Baqir. 1394 SH. "Wakawi-yi ma'nashinakhti-yi 'aql dar zaban 'arabi wa-Qur'an karim ba tikya bar ara' Shaykh Tusi dar al-Tibyan" [A semantic analysis of reason in Arabic and the Holy Quran relying on the opinions of Shaykh Tusi in al-Tibyan]. *Pazhuhish dini*, no. 30:76-84.
19. Sultani Rinani, Muhammad. 1395 SH. "Barrisiyi didgah Shaykh Tusi dar tafsir ayat 'ilm hadith" [A study of Shaykh Tusi's perspective in the exegesis of the verses of the science of hadith]. *Tahqiqat 'ulum Qur'an wa-hadith*, no. 31: 39-62.
20. Fadili, Muhammad and Muhammad Nigarish. 1382 SH. "Nigah balaghi-yi mufassiran bi jumla-hayi khabari dar ayat Qur'an" [Rhetorical perspective of Quranic exegetes on declarative sentences in Quranic verses]. *Mutali'at Islami*, no. 60: 223-248.

4.3.4. Principle of jurisprudence

Books: not found.

Papers

1. Madadi Musawi, Sayyid Muhammad Kazim. 1393 SH. "Sayr tahawwul haml bar taqiyya dar fiqh az dawra-yi Shaykh Tusi ta dawra-yi Muqaddas Ardibili: tahawwul az tariqiyyat bi

mawdu'iyyat" [The evolution of considering as taqiyya in jurisprudence from the period of Shaykh Tusi to the period of Muqaddas Ardabili: a transformation from tariqiyyat to mawdu'iyyat]. *Fiqh*, no. 4: 95-109.

2. Tabataba'ipur, Sayyid Kazim and Hamid Mustafawifard. 1396 SH. "Chigunigi-yi muwajiha-yi Shaykh Tusi ba guftiman Mufid wa-Murtada dar mas'ala-yi hujjiyyat khabar wahid" [How Shaykh Tusi confronts Mufid and Murtada's discourse on the issue of the authority of khabari wahid]. *Fiqh wa-usul*, no. 111: 153-181.

3. 'Abbasi, Firaydun, Mustafa Ahmadifar and Muhammad Imami. 1398 SH. "Rahyafti naw bar hujjiyyat khabar wahid dar tafsir (ba ta'kid bar didgah Shaykh Tusi)" [A new approach to the authority of single-narrator hadiths in Quranic exegesis (with a focus on the view of Shaykh Tusi)]. *Amuzihayi Qur'ani*, no. 29: 251-276.

4.3.5. Political theory

Books

1. Musawian, Muhammad Rida. 1380 SH. *Andisha-yi siyasi-yi Shaykh Tusi* [Political thoughts of Shaykh Tusi]. Qom: Bustan kitab.

2. Musawiyan, Muhammad Rida, Mahmud Shafi'i and 'Ali Khaliqi. 1386 SH. *Nizam siyasi wa-dawlat-i matlub dar andisha-yi siyasi-yi Shaykh Mufid, Sayyid Murtada wa-Shaykh Tusi* [The political system and favorable government in the political thought of Shaykh Mufid, Sayyid Murtada and Shaykh Tusi]. Tehran: Markaz Asnad Inqilab Islami.

Paper

1. Turkashwand, Sajjad and Muhammad Kakawand. 1399 SH. "Mabani-yi fiqhi-yi rujhan masalih 'umumi bar masalih fardi ba muraji'a bi ara' Imam Khomeini wa-Shaykh Tusi" [The

jurisprudential principles of preferring public interests over individual interests by referring to the opinions of Imam Khomeini and Shaykh Tusi]. *Hukumat Islami,* no. 96: 77-100.

4.3.6. On Tusi's wroks

Books

1. Rustami, Haydar ʿAli. 1392 SH. *Barrisi-yi tawsifi tahlili-yi kitab al-Ghayba Shaykh Tusi* [Descriptive and analytical review of the book al-Ghayba by Shaykh Tusi]. Qom: Bustan kitab.
2. Tusi, Muhammad ibn Hasan. 1399 SH. *Fiqh kayfari (tarjuma-yi kitab al-Khilaf fi l-ahkam)* [Criminal jurisprudence (Persian transaltion of the book al-Khilaf fi l-ahkam by Shaykh Tusi]. Translated by Hurmuz Asadi Kuhbadi and ʿAbdulkarim Gulgun. Shiraz: Shahchiragh.
3. Musawi, Mir Mahmud. 1391 SH. *Fihrist asar dastniwis Shaykh al-Ta'ifa Muhammad ibn Hasan Tusi* [List of the manuscripts of Shaykh al-Ta'ifa Muhammad ibn Hasan Tusi in the great Library of Ayatullah Marʿashi Najafi]. Qom: Library of Ayatollah Marʿashi Najafi.
4. Kumpani Zariʿ, Mahdi. 1390 SH. *Shaykh Tusi wa-tafsir Tibyan* [Shaykh Tusi and tafsir Al-Tibyan]. Tehran: Khana-yi Kitab.
5. Safakhah, Muhammad Husayn and ʿAbdulhusiyn Taliʿi. 1380 SH. *Pazhuhishi dar manabiʿ wa-mustanadat tahdhib al-ahkam Shaykh Tusi* [A research into the sources and chains of transmissions of *Tahdhib al-ahkam* by Shaykh Tusi]. Tehran: Abrun.
6. Shaykh Tusi, Muhammad ibn Hasan. 1399 SH. *Amali*. Translated into Persian by Sadiq Hasanzada. Qom: Andisha-yi Hadi.

Papers

1. Hujjati, Muhammad Baqir, Rahin Takfallah and Mahdi Mihrizi Turuqi. 1399 SH. "I'tibarsanji-yi riwayat kitab Misbah al-mujtahid wa-silah al-muta'abbid" [Validation of the hadiths of the book Misbah al-mutahajjid wa-silah al-muta'abbid]. *Pazhuhishnama-yi Imamyya*, no. 12: 80-108.

2. Adabi Mihar, Muhammad. 1384 SH. "Pazhuhishi piramun musanifat Shaykh Tusi" [A research on Shaykh Tusi's writings]. *Pazhuhish dini*, no. 12: 129-150.

3. Jalali, Mahdi and Rahima Shamshiri. 1387 SH. "Barrisi-yi rawish 'umumi Shaykh Tusi dar kitab al-Fihrist" [A study of the general method of Shaykh Tusi in the book *al-Fihrist*]. *'Ulum Qur'an wa-hadith*, no. 81:135-164.

4. Kazim, Tabataba'i and 'Illiyya Ridadad. 1387 SH. "Gahshumari-yi asar Shaykh Tusi" [Chronology of Shaykh Tusi›s works]. *Mutali'at Islami*, no. 80: 49-73.

5. Jalali, Mahdi and Rahima Shamshiri. 1388 SH. "Mazayayi Fihrist Najashi bar Fihrist wa-Rijal Shaykh Tusi wa-barrisiyi nisbat wa-ikhtilaf anha ba yikdigar" [The advantages of Najashi's *al-Fihrist* over Shaykh Tusi's *al-Fihrist* and *Rijal* and examining their relationship and differences with each other]. *'Ulum Qur'an wa-hadith*, no. 83: 101-120.

6. Surkha'i, Ihsan. 1395 SH. "Karburd lah riwayat dar *Fihrist* Shaykh Tusi wa-irtibat an ba kutub nawadir" [The function of "lah riwayat" in Shaykh Tusi's *Fihrist* and its relation with kutub nawadir]. *'Ulum hadith*, no. 81: 98-125.

7. Mihrizi, Mahdi and Zahra Hasani. 1391 SH. "Guzarishi az tahlil madamin ad'iya mah rajab bar asas misbah al-mujtahid Shaykh Tusi" [A report on the analysis of the contents of the prayers of the

month of Rajab based on Misbah al-mutihajjid Shaykh Tusi]. *'Ulum hadith*, no. 64:160-180.

8. 'Arabi, Nasim. 1397 SH. "Rahyaft istiqra'i bar adabiyyat ijtihadi-yi kitab al-Khilaf" [Inductive approach to the ijtihad literature of the book *al-Khilaf*]. *Pazhuhishnama-yi madhahib Islami*, no. 10:227-248.

4.3.7. On Tusi's life

Books

1. Yusifzada, Hasan. 1398 SH. *Majmu'a musahiba-hayi bistumin jashnwara-yi baynalmilali-yi pazhuhishi Shaykh Tusi* [The collection of interviews of the 20th Shaykh Tusi International Research Festival]. Qom: Al-Musta International Center for Translation and Publication.
2. Kumpani Zari', Mahdi. 1392 SH. *Tusi pazhuhi (majmu'a maqalati dar barrisi-yi ara', ahwal wa-athar Shaykh Tusi)* [Research on Tusi (Collection of articles on the study of the opinions, circumstances and works of Shaykh Tusi)]. Tehran: Khana Kitab.
3. Haydari Malikmiyan, Firaydun. 1391 SH. *Shaykh Tusi*. Tehran: Mu'assasa-yi Farhangi-yi Madrisa-yi Burhan.
4. Shahruwi, 'Alirida. 1374 SH. *Al-Tusi Shaykh al-Ta'ifa*. Translated by Kamal Sayyid. Qom: Ansarian.
5. Shahruwi, 'Alirida. 1382 SH. *Shaykh Tusi khurshid abrar*. Tehran: Shirkat Chap wa-Nashr Bayn al-Milal.
6. Kumpani Zari', Mahdi. 1395 SH. *Shaykh Tusi pishwa-yi 'aliman shi'i* [Shaykh Tusi, the leader of Shiite Scholars]. Tehran: Waya.
7. Aqa Buzurg Tihrani, Muhammad Muhsin. 1360 SH. *Zindiginama-yi Shaykh Tusi* [The biography of Shaykh Tusi]. Translated by 'Alirida

Mirzamuhammad and Hamid Tabibiyan. Tehran: Farhangistan Adab wa-Hunar.

Papers

1. Manzur al-Ajdad, Muhammad Husayn. 1381 SH. "Shurish basasiri wa-payamad-hayi an barayi Shiʿayan Baghdad" [The Basasiri riot and its consequences for Shiites of Baghdad]. *Zaban wa-adabiyyat Farsi*, no, 35-39: 87-110.

2. Ridazada ʿAskari, Zahra. 1384 SH. "Naqsh Shaykh Tusi dar ijad nihdat ʿilmi ba taʾkid bar tatawwur fiqhi" [Shaykh Tusi's role in creating a scientific movement with a focus on jurisprudential evolution]. *Pazhuhish dini*, no. 12: 235-250.

3. Kariminiya, Murtada. 1385 SH. "Shaykh Tusi wa-manabiʿ tafsiri-yi way dar al-Tibyan" [Shaykh Tusi and exegetical principles in al-Tibyan]. *Mutaliʿat Islami*, no. 74: 81-111.

4. Kazim, Ustadi. 1400 SH. "Barrisi-yi intisab sanad kitab Sulaym bi Shaykh Tusi" [Investigating the attribution of the chain of transmission of Salim's Book to Shaykh Tusi]. *ʿUlum hadith*, no. 99: 150-177.

4.3.8. Ethics

Books: not found.

Paper

1. Pashaʾi, Wahid, Hadi Sadiqi and Husayn Zariʿ. 1398 SH. "Mabani maʿrifat shinakhti-yi akhlaqi dar andisha-yi kalami Shaykh Tusi" [Epistemological principles of ethics in the theological thought of Shaykh Tusi]. *Tahqiqat kalami*, no. 27: 85-102.

4.3.9. Literature

Books: not found.

Paper

1. Fadili, Muhammad and Muhammad Nigarish. 1382 SH. "Nigah balaghi-yi mufassiran bi jumla-hayi khabari dar ayat Qur'an" [Rhetorical perspective of Quranic exegetes on declarative sentences in Quranic Verses]. *Mutali'at Islami*, no. 60: 223-248.

2. Qurbani Zarrin, Baqir. 1394 SH. "Wakawi-yi ma'nashinakhti 'aql dar zaban 'arabi wa-Qur'an karim ba tikya bar ara' Shaykh Tusi dar al-Tibyan" [Semantic analysis of reason in Arabic and the Holy Quran relying on the opinions of Shaykh Tusi in *al-Tibyan*]. *Pazhuhish dini*, no. 30: 76-84.

3. Baqir, 'Alirida and Fatima 'Amiri. 1397 SH. "Naqsh 'ulum balaghi dar tafsir Qur'an (mutali'a-yi mawridi-yi kinaya wa ta'rid dar tafsir tibyan Shaykh Tusi wa-Kashshaf Zamakhshari" [The role of rhetorical sciences in Quranic exegesis (a case study of irony and sarcasm in Shaykh Tusi's tafsir al-Tibyan and Zamakhshari's Kashshaf)]. *Pazhuhishhayi tafsir tatbiqi*, no. 8: 39-63.

4. Kazimi Sahliwani, Hasan, Ghulam 'Abbas Rida'i Haftadari and Ibrahim Dibaji. 1393 SH. "Ma'nashinasi Qur'an dar tafsir Tibyan Shaykh Tusi" [The semantics of the Qur'an in Shaykh Tusi's tafsir al-Tibyan]. *'Uyun*, no. 1: 25-38.

5. Rida'i Haftadar, Ghulam 'Abbas, Ibrahim Dibaji and Hasan Kazimi Sahliwani. 1396 SH. "Barrisi-yi ma'nashinasi wazha-yi salam dar tafsir Tibyan Shaykh Tusi" [A study of the semantics of the word salam in Shaykh Tusi's tafsir al-Tibyan]. *Adab 'Arabi*, no.1: 249-260.

6. 'Amari Allahyari, Zahra and Shadi Nafisi. 1393 SH. "Mabani-yi ruykard adabi dar tafsir Murtada wa-Shaykh Tusi ba ta'kid bar al-

Amali wa-al-Tibyan" [Principles of literary approach in the exegesis of Siyyid Murtiża and Shaykh Tusi based on al-Amali and al-Tibyan]. *Pazhuhishhayi Adabi Qur'ani*, no. 3: 103-137.

7. Farid, Zahra and Amir Mahmud Anwar. 1392 SH. "Ruykard lughawi Shaykh Tusi dar Tafsir Tibyan" [Shaykh Tusi's lexical approach in tafsir al-Tibyan]. *Lisan mubin*, no. 11: 18-36.

Appendix: selected photos of the classical manuscripts of Tusi's works

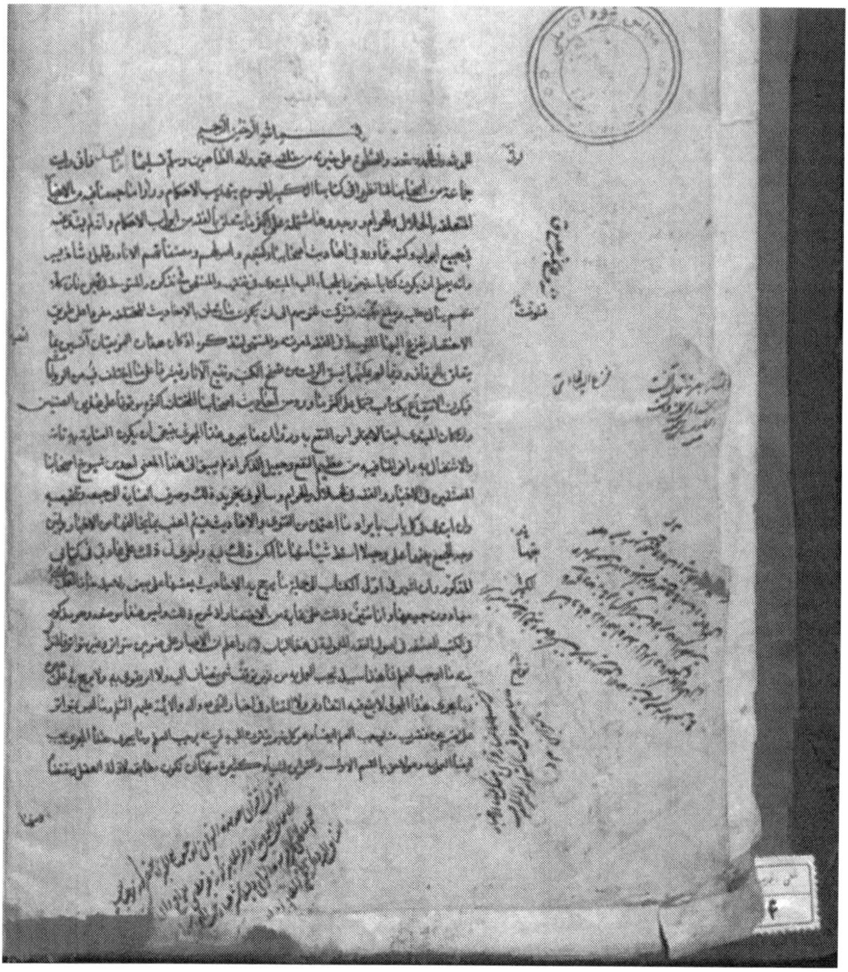

Al-Istibṣār fī-mā ikhtalaf min al-akhbār

Page number: 417 sheets

Recovery no.: Khoei 14

Archiving place: Library of Majlis

Date of transcription: Eleventh century

Transcriber: unknown

Al-Ghayba

Page number: 392 pages

Recovery no.: 1949

Archiving place: Library of Feyziyeh School

Date of transcription: Tuesday Ramadan 5, 1085 (December 3, 1674)

Transcriber: Khafal ibn Yūsuf ibn Najm al-Najafī

Al-Istibṣār fī-mā ikhtalaf min al-akhbār

Page number: 393 pages

Recovery no.: 13679

Archiving place: Library of Ayatollah Marʿashī Najafī

Date of transcription: Safar 569 AH (September/October, 1173)

Transcriber: Muḥammad ibn al-Ḥasan ibn Muḥammad ibn al-ʿAbbās Nāzawayh

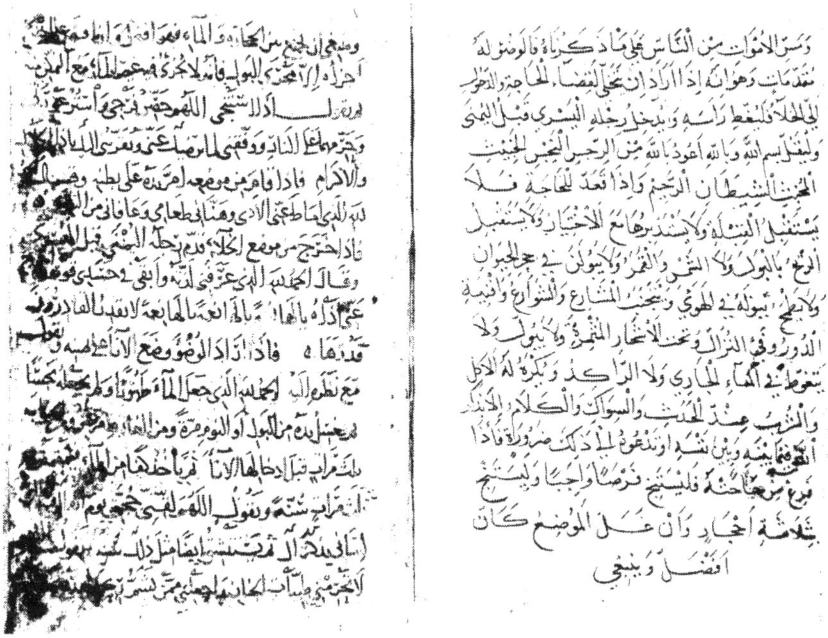

Miṣbāḥ al-mutahajjid fī ʿamal al-sunna

Page number: 263 pages

Recovery no.: 13241

Archiving place: Library of Ayatollah Marʿashī Najafī

Date of transcription: First half of the sixth century AH (first half of the twelfth century CE)

Transcriber: unknown

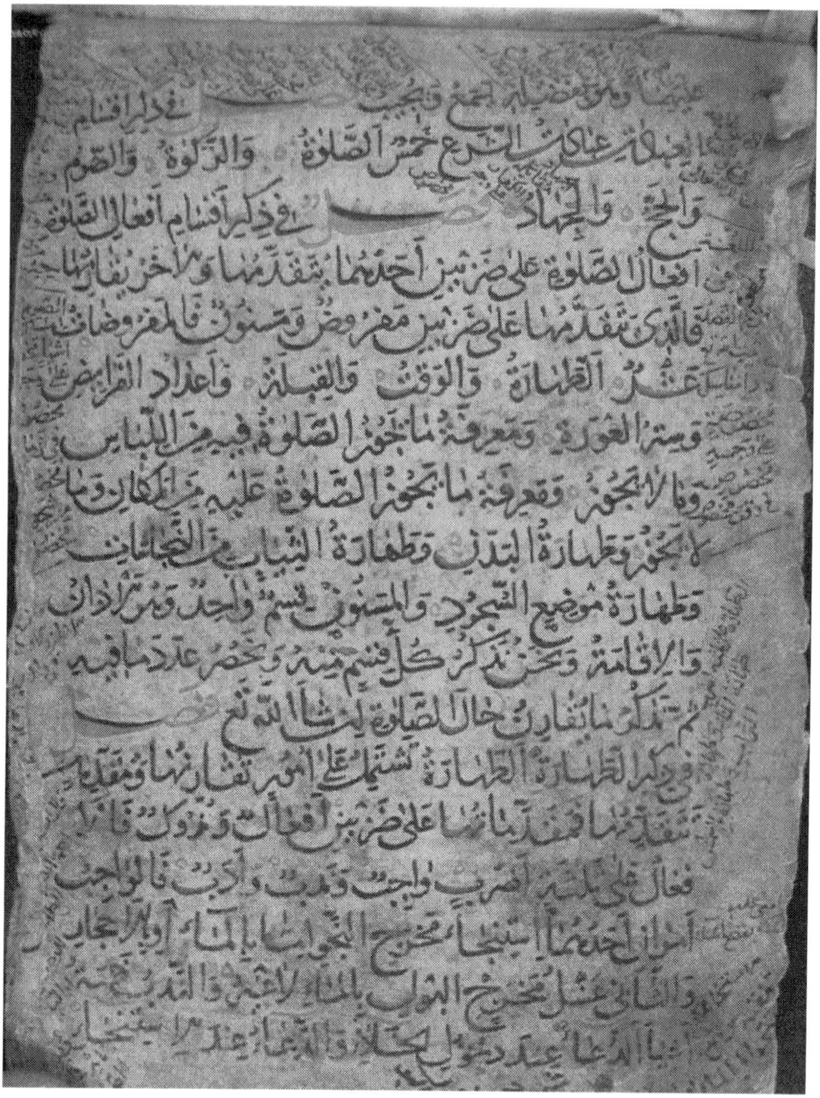

Al-Jumal wa-l-ʿuqūd fi l-ʿibādāt

Page number: 42 sheets

Recovery no.: 1/534

Archiving place: Library of Ferdowsi University of Mashhad (College of Theology)

Date of transcription: Dhu l-Qaʿdah 1, 691 AH (October 14, 1291)

Transcriber: Ḥusayn ibn Aḥmad Mashshāṭ Āmulī, known as Ḥakīm

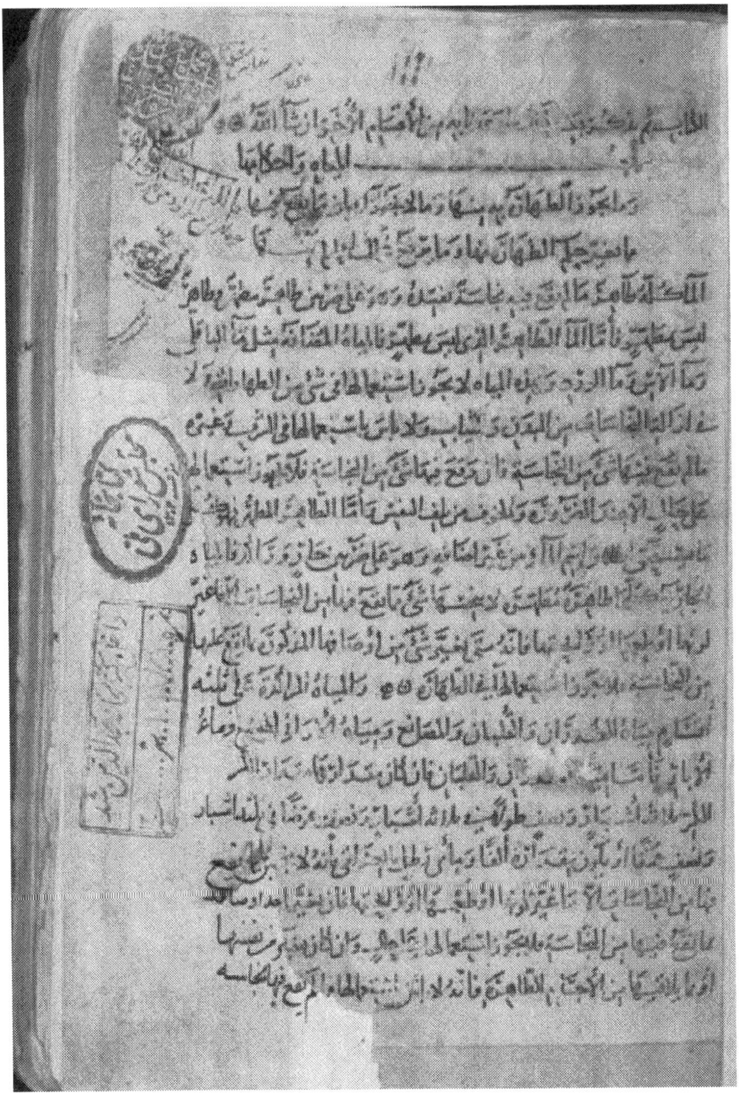

Al-nihāya fī mujarrad al-fiqh wa-l-fatāwā

number: 485 pages

Recovery no.: 2727

Archiving place: Library of Majlis

Date of transcription: Saturday, Ramadan 15, 699 AH (June 4, 1300)

Transcriber: Muḥammad ibn Mahyār Ḥasan ibn Ḥusayn ibn ʿAlī al-Hirqilī

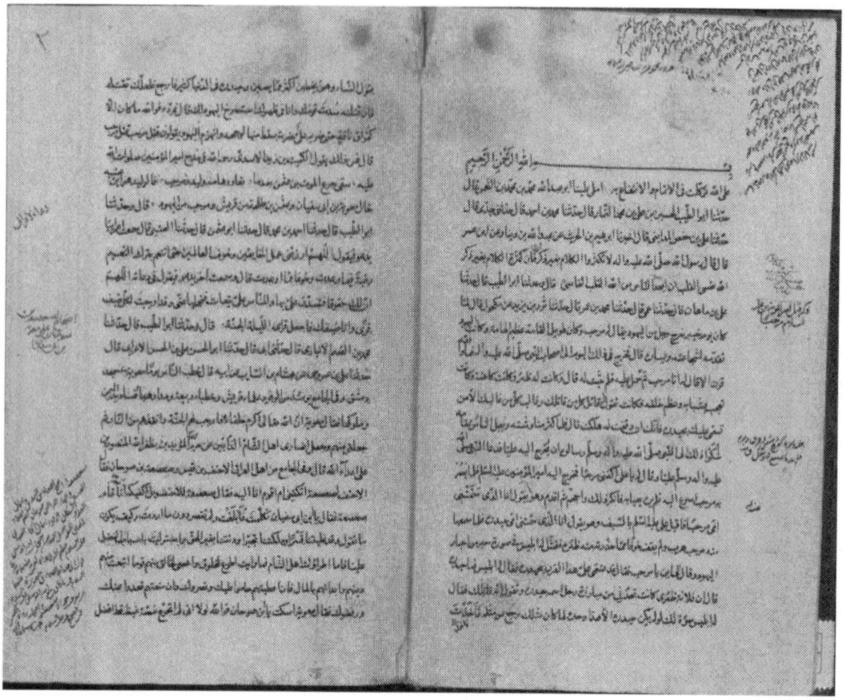

Al-Majālis fi l-akhbār

number: 180 sheets

Recovery no.: 7112

Archiving place: Library of Majlis

Date of transcription: Saturday, Sha'ban 22, 1075 AH (March 10, 1665)

Transcriber: Muḥammad Mu'min al-Abharī al-Ḥayy Iṣfahān ibn Muḥammad ibn Mīrzā 'Alī

Made in the USA
Middletown, DE
16 July 2023

34562114R00109